The Lord's Prayer in Matthew 6:9–13

THE LORD'S PRAYER IN MATTHEW 6:9–13

A Socio-rhetorical Analysis of Identity Politics
of the Matthean Community

F. Manjewa M'bwangi

◆PICKWICK *Publications* • Eugene, Oregon

THE LORD'S PRAYER IN MATTHEW 6:9–13
A Socio-rhetorical Analysis of Identity Politics of the Matthean Community

Copyright © 2022 F. Manjewa M'bwangi. All rights reserved. Except for brief quotations in critical publications or reviews, no part of this book may be reproduced in any manner without prior written permission from the publisher. Write: Permissions, Wipf and Stock Publishers, 199 W. 8th Ave., Suite 3, Eugene, OR 97401.

Pickwick Publications
An Imprint of Wipf and Stock Publishers
199 W. 8th Ave., Suite 3
Eugene, OR 97401

www.wipfandstock.com

PAPERBACK ISBN: 978-1-6667-1018-2
HARDCOVER ISBN: 978-1-6667-1019-9
EBOOK ISBN: 978-1-6667-1020-5

Cataloguing-in-Publication data:

Names: M'bwangi, F. Manjewa, author.

Title: The Lord's Prayer in Matthew 6:9–13 : a socio-rhetorical analysis of identity politics of the matthean community / by F. Manjewa M'bwangi.

Description: Eugene, OR: Pickwick Publications, 2022 | Includes bibliographical references and index.

Identifiers: ISBN 978-1-6667-1018-2 (paperback) | ISBN 978-1-6667-1019-9 (hardcover) | ISBN 978-1-6667-1020-5 (ebook)

Subjects: LCSH: Bible. Matthew, VI, 9–13—Socio-rhetorical criticism. | Lord's prayer—Criticism, interpretation, etc. | Identification (Religion)—Biblical teaching.

Classification: BV230 M393 2022 (print) | BV230 (ebook)

04/22/22

This book, *The Lord's Prayer in Matthew 6:9-13: A Socio rhetorical Analysis of the Identity Politics of the Matthean Community* is voluntarily dedicated to the Anglican Diocese of Mombasa, Kenya. Any financial proceeds realized through the sale of this book will be paid directly to the Anglican Diocese of Mombasa for the purpose of supporting church ministry at the discretion of the Bishop of the Anglican Diocese of Mombasa.

CONTENTS

PREFACE | ix
ACKNOWLEDGMENTS | xi
LIST OF ABBREVIATIONS | xiii

INTRODUCTION | 1

CHAPTER 1: BRIEF TRENDS IN NEW TESTAMENT SCHOLARSHIP | 3
    1.1 Tilborg   3
    1.2 Nel   4
    1.3 Drake   7

CHAPTER 2: A SOCIO-RHETORICAL ANALYTIC THEORY | 9
    2.1 Vernon K. Robbins's Socio-rhetorical Interpretation   9
    2.2 Ideological Analysis   12
    2.3 Identity Politics Analysis   15
    2.4 Conclusion   20

CHAPTER 3: SEMANTIC ANALYSIS OF MATTHEW 6:9–13 | 22
    3.1 Inner Textual Analysis   22
        3.1.1 Repetitive-Progressive Inner Texture   22
        3.1.2 Opening-Middle-Closing Inner Texture   26
        3.1.3 Narrational Inner Texture   30
    3.2 Conclusion   33

CHAPTER 4: THE SOCIAL SETTING | 34
    4.1 Antioch: Geographical and Sociological Composition of Matthew's Community   34
    4.2 Identity in Rome, Diaspora Judaism, and the Jesus Movement   41

CONTENTS

- 4.2.1 Trends in New Testament Scholarship regarding Roman Empire 42
- 4.2.2 Identity Formation in the Roman Empire 45
- 4.2.3 Negotiating of Judaean Hybrid Identity in the Diaspora 65
- 4.2.4 Identity Construction and Maintenance in the Jesus Movement 83

4.3 Conclusion 97

CHAPTER 5: MATTHEW 6:9–13 AND CONSTRUCTION OF IDENTITY POLITICS | 98

5.1 Cultural, Social, and Historical Perspectives 98
- 5.1.1 Cultural Perspective 98
- 5.1.2 Social Perspective 100
- 5.1.3 Historical Perspective 101

5.2 Reconstruction and Legitimation of a Christian Identity 104
- 5.2.1 Baasland 104
- 5.2.2 DuToit 104
- 5.2.3 Reconstructing a Christian Cultural Identity through Recategorization 106
- 5.2.4. Legitimating a Christian Identity through Identification 110

5.3 A Social-Evangelistic Identity Politics 114
- 5.3.1 Accommodating Jewish Tradition to Encourage Non-violent Attitude 114
- 5.3.2 Identification with Israel to Advocate for Social Good 115
- 5.3.3 Appropriating Jesus' Prayers to Promote an Inclusive Household 116

5.4 Conclusion 117

CHAPTER 6: CONCLUSION | 118

BIBLIOGRAPHY | 121
SUBJECT INDEX | 129
ANCIENT SOURCES INDEX | 143

PREFACE

New Testament scholars have long grappled with the origin and semantic function of the Lord's Prayer in Matthew 6:9–13. Some scholars describe Matthew's Lord's Prayer either as reflective of an ideological intervention, enjoining the remission of every exploitative debt or that it commands debt and sin forgiveness. However, these scholars do not elaborate their understanding of Matthew's Lord's Prayer from the standpoint of its connection with Matthew's concept of righteousness and its socio-economic and political connectedness to the world of the Roman Empire and the Jesus Movement. In this book I will attempt to answer the question: how does Matthew use his version of the Lord's Prayer to elaborate the rhetorical function of his concept of righteousness in shaping the identity of his community in the late first century CE? In a wider literary context (6:1–18), Matthew 6:1 indicates that Jesus required from his followers a certain type of righteousness that was not directed at achieving honor via others. This type of righteousness led Jesus to teach his disciples to recite the Lord's Prayer as expressive of the righteousness approved by him. In this book, I argue that Matthew employs his version of the Lord's Prayer to recategorize his community into a superordinate identity through identification with Jewish religious traditions, through contesting Roman political and economic claims of benefices, and through accommodating the liturgical traditions of the Jesus Movement. The goal of analyzing this recategorization comparison, accommodation and identification is to explain the role of the Matthean Lord's Prayer in elaborating identity politics of the Matthean community in the Roman Empire. In the process, the ideological function of Matthew's concept of righteousness will be elaborated in reference to socio-economic and political context of the Roman Empire, post-70 CE Diaspora Judaism, and the Jesus Movement in late first century CE. This book helps us to explore Matthew's rhetorical application of the concept of righteousness as a hermeneutical key that reveals Matthew's ideology in his Gospel narrative. In this study, the blending of Vernon K. Robbins's socio-rhetorical interpretation with social scientific concepts of recategorization, contestation, accommodation, identification and social evangelism movement, demonstrate interdisciplinary approach to religious studies, particularly Biblical studies.

ACKNOWLEDGMENTS

THIS PUBLICATION OF THE monograph, *The Lord's Prayer in Matthew 6:9-13: A Socio-rhetorical Analysis of Identity Politics of the Matthean Community*, would not have been completed without the support of some individuals and institutions that believed in my dream and wanted to see its realization come to pass. To this end, I am obliged to register my most heartfelt gratitude to Pwani University Board of Management for granting me a two year leave of absence (15th February 2020 to 15th January 2022) to pursue a Post-Doctoral Research Fellowship at the University of Pretoria, Republic of South Africa. Equally important is my indebtedness to the role of the University of Cape Town, particularly the Department of Religious Studies for providing workshops and seminars that helped to gradually conceptualize area of research and acquire research and writing skills necessary for the realization of my PhD thesis. I cannot forget the crucial role of the Council for the Development of Social Sciences Research in Africa (CODESRIA) and the National Institute for the Humanities and Social Sciences (NIHSS) for jointly awarding me a four-year African Pathways Scholarship (2015–18) that provided the tuition fees and stipend that collectively bolstered psychological peace that was crucial to the realization of my PhD Thesis from which this book is derived. I cannot forget to appreciate the contributions of my two PhD supervisors at UCT, Associate Professor Charles A. Wanamaker and Dr. Louis Blond, who, in a relationship I describe as a "collegial cooperation" provided a friendly but academically strict atmosphere that saw the development of my PhD research project through several phases. A most precious gratitude goes to Dr. Zorodzai Dube, a Senior Lecturer in the Department of New Testament and Related Literatures, University of Pretoria, for accepting to play the crucial role of a Mentor during my Post-Doctoral Research Fellowship at the University of Pretoria which has materialized to the production of this

ACKNOWLEDGMENTS

book and other several articles published in double-blind peer reviewed journals. Finally, my heartfelt appreciation goes to Rachel McIntyre, the Registrar at the Oxford Center for Mission Studies (OCMS), for guiding me to contact Pickwick Publications, an imprint of Wipf and Stock Publishers, to ask them to consider publishing this book.

ABBREVIATIONS

AJ	Josephus, *Antiquity of the Jews*
BCE	Before Common Era
BDAG	Bauer, Walter, et al. *A Greek-English Lexicon of the New Testament and Early Christian Literature.*
BJ	Josephus, *Wars of the Jews*
CE	Common Era
NA28	*Novum Testamentum Graece* (Nestle-Aland). 28th ed.
Neot	*Neotestamentica*
NIV	New International Version
NovTest	*Novum Testamentum*
NRSV	New Revised Standard Version
NTS	*New Testament Studies*
SM	Sermon on the Mount
SRAT	Socio-rhetorical Analysis Theory
SRI	Socio-rhetorical Interpretation
WUNT	Wissenschaftliche Untersuchungen zum Neuen Testament

INTRODUCTION

THE TITLE OF THIS book, *The Lord's Prayer in Matthew 6:9–13: A Socio-rhetorical Analysis of Identity Politics of the Matthean Community*, points to the subject matter being addressed in this book. Although literary approaches such as form, redaction, source criticisms have been employed to analyze the text of the Gospel of Matthew to discuss the theological significance of Matthew's version of the Lord's Prayer, little has been done in exploring the Lord's Prayer as a reflection of the social concerns of the community of Matthew in the late first century, particularly the identity politics of the community reflected in the text. By employing socio-rhetorical analysis theory to read Matthew 6:9–13 not only do I use social scientific concepts derived from socio-rhetorical interpretation and ideological analysis to describe the identity politics reflected in Matthew's Lord's Prayer, but also to describe the group relations of the community of Matthew with the Roman Empire, Diaspora Judaism and the Jesus Movement (members of early Christian communities) in the geographical and sociological location of Syrian Antioch city in the late first century CE. Notably, the exploration of late first century CE social setting in order to describe the group-relations of the Community of Matthew in effect reveals the importance of using sociological and anthropological perspectives to discuss Matthew's version of the Lord's Prayer. In this case, we regard sociology as the study of the development, structure, and functioning of human society and anthropology as the study of systems, such as of knowledge, within particular cultures.[1] The qualitative research methods and writing skills I acquired during my four-year (2015–19) PhD research project at the University of Cape Town (Republic of South Africa), which primarily explored a strategy of

---

1. Kempny, "Cultural Context," 15.

exegesis that blends literary analysis with social sciences to explore the discourse of early Christian communities, enabled me to critically read the hermeneutical function of Matthew's concept of righteousness as an ideology for describing the identity politics of his community.

Consequently, by reading this book, not only will you be briefly introduced to some of the current trends of research regarding the Lord's Prayer in Matthew's Gospel that provide the backdrop to the knowledge gap addressed in this book, but you will also explore modern interpretive dynamics that utilize social scientific models to read the Lord's Prayer, and by large the New Testament texts. Thus, the book is relevant for undergraduate and post-graduates students, researchers and pastors seeking to familiarize themselves with how literary analysis (inner texture and inter texture) can be blended with social scientific concepts (ideology and identity politics) to read texts, for instance, the biblical text as refelction of the discourse of the early Christian communities. To this end, chapter 1 introduces you to some trends in the New Testament research regarding the Lord's Prayer in Matthew 6:9–13. Chapter two explores the tenets of the Socio-rhetorical Analysis Theory (SRAT) to prepare you with rhetorical epistemological perspectives and skills for doing a semantic analysis of Matthew 6:9–13 discussed in chapter three. Chapter four addresses the social setting of the late first century CE in reference to the identity formation in the Roman Empire, Diaspora Judaism and the Jesus Movement as a backdrop to the emergence of Matthew's version of the Lord's Prayer which he used to construct the identity politics for his community in Antioch in the late first century CE, issues which are addressed in chapter five, before the conclusion in Chapter six.

CHAPTER I

BRIEF TRENDS IN NEW TESTAMENT SCHOLARSHIP

To set the current findings of this study in the on-going context of New Testament scholarship, I shall briefly examine the research works of Sjef van Tilborg, Marius J. Nel, and Lyndon Drake regarding the semantic function of Matthew's Lord's Prayer. The purpose of this brief survey is to find the gap of knowledge regarding the role of Matthean Lord's Prayer, which opens the door to the contribution of this book in Matthean scholarship.

1.1 Tilborg

Tilborg employs Althusser's philosophical theory of ideology to analyze the Gospel of Matthew and defend his argument that the individual sayings of the SM (Sermon on the Mount) are always seen as ideological intervention in the context of an existing social practice.[1] Tilborg further claims that the Lord' Prayer is an ideological intervention, because it opens the way to envision the connection between mythology and ideology as understood by Matthew.[2] Tilborg raises three main categories within this claim: place, time and remittance of economic debts. First, regarding place, Tilborg claims that because of the phrase Πάτερ ἡμῶν ὁ ἐν τοῖς οὐρανοῖς (our father who is in the heavens) in Matt 6:9, the prayer creates opposition between two places—the heavens as the mythological place of God, and the earth as a place where men who recite this prayer live.[3] Second, with regards to time; because the prayer is reformulated to and personified in the concept of "our Father who is in the heavens,"

1. Tilborg, *Sermon on the Mount*, 1.
2. Tilborg, *Sermon on the Mount*, 41.
3. Tilborg, *Sermon on the Mount*, 116.

the prayer connects the mythological transcendence of God and the presence of those who recite the prayer to emphasize the nearness of family relationships, group determinants, and group exclusion.[4] Third, because ἄφες ἡμῖν τὰ ὀφειλήματα ἡμῶν (forgive us our debts) in 6:12, a reference to remittance of "debt," is set in the context of the financial condition of the Matthean community, it prevents us from taking refuge too quickly in the spiritual sense of forgiveness and enjoins us to forgive our neighbor's debts as the condition for receiving God's forgiveness.[5] It is noteworthy here that Tilborg rightly sees Matthew's ideological connection between sin-forgiveness and debt-cancellation as an aspect of empowerment to the community. However, Tilborg ignores two important aspects of the prayer. On the one hand, he does not clarify how the group determinant and group exclusion regarding the petition "our Father who art in the heavens" (Matt 6:9) points to identity formation. Tilborg also does not tell us whether the cancellation of debts in 6:12 refers to all or only some types of debts. However, Nel addresses this ambiguity on the types of debts.

1.2 Nel

Nel, using a combination of socio-historical approach, literary theory and argumentative textual analysis, attends to the question; "whether the fifth petition of the Lord's Prayer (Matt 6:12) considers the remission of the monetary debt of others as a precondition for receiving the forgiveness from God."[6] Advancing beyond Tilborg's failure not to elaborate or state the importance of the connection between the forgiveness of sin and debt cancellation, Nel rightly asserts that answering the question of debt and forgiveness in the Lord's Prayer helps to understand the socio-economic ethics of Matthew's gospel regarding debt and interpersonal relations.[7] Thus, on the question of the relationship between forgiveness and debts, Nel claims that

> while the demand for the remission of every exploitative debt [or all moral transgression] would fit Matthew's monetary demand for righteousness (Matt 6:33), the remission of all monetary debts

4. Tilborg, *Sermon on the Mount*, 130.
5. Tilborg, "Form-Criticism," 122.
6. Nel, "Forgiveness of Debt," 87.
7. Nel, "Forgiveness of Debt," 87, 90–94.

does not, as Jesus neither forbade loans nor demanded a cancellation of every debt.[8]

Nel grounds his claim on three premises: the historical context of prosbul, the rejection of the Jubilee year interpretative lens, and the semantic role of debt in the narrative. First, Nel suggests that the prosbul, a pharisaic doctrine practiced in Palestine and Syria that transferred debts to the law courts to be paid beyond the Sabbatical Year, points to the cancellation of exploitative debt, but not all debt, fitting Matthew's demand for righteousness.[9] Second, he disputes the Jubilee interpretative context for Matthew 6:12 for three reasons: (1) Nel claims that Matthew 6:12 does not refer to Leviticus 25, where the details of the Jubilee year are set out, but instead it refers to Isaiah 61:1–7, "the release of prisoners without specifying that they were held captive because of debts." (2) Nel further claims that when Matt 6:12 is considered in relation to Matthew 18:23–35, it stresses forgiveness of the people to whom one is indebted, unlike the Jubilee year in the Hebrew Bible which refers only to the release of debtors from their own debt.[10] (3) Engaging Jubilee to interpret Matthew 6:12, Nel says that forgiveness needs to refer to cancellation of all debts instead of only exploitative debts.[11] Matthew 5:25–26 envisions a conflicting understanding in which debt repayment is required without cancellation.[12]

Nel advances the findings of Tilborg on two fronts. First, he does this through an argumentative analysis that rejects the Jubilee year as a hermeneutical key for interpreting the Lord's Prayer. Nel rejects the notion that the Jubilee year provided a reason to justify the demands for remission of debts in Matthew's Lord's Prayer. Nel claims that regarding the Jubilee as a motivation to remit exploitative debts could lead to the misinterpretation that the fifth petition of the Lord's Prayer as "demanding the unqualified forgiveness of all monetary debts," an idea not supported in Matthew's narrative.[13] Second, Nel contends that it is the motif of reciprocity in Matt 6:14–15, instead of the Jubilee year, that fits as the hermeneutical key for interpreting the forgiveness of debt. By this suggestion, Nel elaborates

8. Nel, "Forgiveness of Debt," 102.
9. Nel, "Forgiveness of Debt," 90–93.
10. Nel, "Forgiveness of Debt," 92.
11. Nel, "Forgiveness of Debt," 92.
12. Nel, "Forgiveness of Debt," 94.
13. Nel, "Forgiveness of Debt," 92–93, 102–3.

Tilborg's view of righteousness in 6:1 as the hermeneutical key for explaining the fifth petition of the Lord's Prayer.

By appealing to the socio-historical context of the Matthean community to reconstruct its social-economic status in first century CE Palestine and Syria, not only does Nel engage social history as a lens to study the Lord's Prayer, but he also reconstructs the underlying social issues such as *prosbul* (transfer of personal loans by rich land owners to a law court so as to remain repayable even after a Sabbatical Year). Moreover, by this approach, Nel presents the Matthean community as a wealthy urban community. He also effectively presents the argumentative function of Matthew 6:14–15, which allows Nel to elaborate Tilborg's view of the fifth petition. This elaboration is based on Nel's conclusion that the fifth petition indicates that "while a demand for the remission of every exploitative debt . . . would fit Matthew's demand for righteousness (6:33), the remission of all monetary debts does not, as Jesus neither forbade loans, nor demanded the cancellation of every debt, nor the rebellion against exploitative economic practices in the Matthean Parables" (Matt 5:25–26, 40, 42; 18:23–35).[14]

From this brief investigation, two crucial points are observable. First, we see that Nel does not regard the Lord's Prayer as an ideological intervention as Tilborg does. Nonetheless, Nel's assertion that the fifth petition (Matt 6:12) demands the remission of every exploitative debt that fits Matthew's demands for righteousness inadvertently supports the understanding of the fifth petition as an ideological intervention in support of the poor or marginalized, by suppressing the forces of oppression in the first century CE Palestinian and Syrian society.[15] Even though Nel connects forgiveness to Matthew's righteousness, unfortunately he rejects the interpretive role of the Biblical Jubilee in expounding the Matthean notion of forgiveness of sins and debts. In the year of Jubilee, it was declared to all Hebrews: "And you shall hallow the fiftieth year and you shall proclaim liberty throughout the land to all its inhabitants. It shall be a jubilee for you: you shall return, every one of you, to your property and every one of you to your family" (Lev 25:10 NRSV). So, I argue that both the Jubilee, as a crucial tradition for Israelite identity, and the Prosbul, a Pharisaic invention, positively and negatively motivated the cancellation of exploitative debt in Matthew's community, respectively.

---

14. Nel, "Forgiveness of Debt," 102.
15. Tilborg, "Form-Criticism," 102.

This declaration of Jubilee to Hebrews guaranteed that those who had sold themselves as slaves to their fellow Hebrews would gain freedom. Thus, inter-textually, forgiveness in Matt 6:12 mimicked the year of Jubilee to grant forgiveness that had an economic dimension in that it allowed people to repossess the land. It also had a social dimension, because such forgiveness reconciled those who had been slaves to their families. Consequently, such forgiveness would automatically mitigate the excess of *prosbul* upon the people by restoring economic liberty to them, which was denied by the Jewish elites or aristocrats under the *prosbul arrangements*. Besides Nel, the other person that addresses the issue of forgiveness in Matt 6:12 is Lyndon Drake.

1.3 Drake

Drake engages inter-textual and discourse analysis to study forgiveness in the Matthean Lord's Prayer. Contrary to Nel, Drake argues that, "the historical Jesus chose the terminology of debt to enjoin his followers to forgive monetary debts, as well as sins."[16] Why did Jesus join sin and debt in his prayer? Drake argues that Jesus connected the two to oppose the Pharisaic innovation of the *prosbul*. This connection rhetorically subverted the economic significance of the Jubilee year (Deut 15:1–6; Exod 21:2–6; 23:10–11; Isa 61:1; Jer 34:8–17; Ezek 46:17). Drake briefly points out three reasons besides opposition of the prosbul to justify his argument. First, in 6:12, the prayer is asking for God's forgiveness based on having already forgiven our own debtors (ἡμεῖς ἀφήκαμεν τοῖς ὀφειλέταις ἡμῶν). Thus, a comparison is created between "small forgiveness/release practiced by Jesus's followers that included all kinds of debts: money, obligation and sins, to a larger forgiveness/release that only God can wield."[17] Second, inter textually, Josephus (*BJ* 2.427) claims that the Jewish revolt against Rome in 66–73 CE was partly caused by the prosbul that had contributed to the debt crisis which ignited the revolt. Third, the wider literary context of the SM (5:12; 6:19–24) suggests that the Matthean redactor understood Jesus to have debt in view as well as sin.[18] Consequently, Drake claims that Matthew added the clarifying statement

---

16. Drake, "Did Jesus Oppose the *Prosbul*?," 233.
17. Drake, "Did Jesus Oppose the *Prosbul*?," 234.
18. Drake, "Did Jesus Oppose the *Prosbul*?," 240.

in 6:14–15, "to ensure that all intended readers would understand that 'debt' in prayer includes sin as well as money debts."[19]

Because Nel and Drake seem to agree that forgiveness in Matthew 6:12 was intended to prohibit the exploitative application of *prosbul*, they imply that Matthew composed the Lord's Prayer to address the economic injustices of the common person by the Judean elite in Syrian Antioch in the late first-century CE. Drake and Nel's make a similar suggestion that Matt 6:14–15 provides the leverage for explaining the semantic function of the Matthean Lord's Prayer, particularly the fifth petition. Contrary to Nel and Drake and in support of Tilborg, Matthew's use of righteousness, particularly in 5:20 and 6:1–33, provides the leverage not only for explaining the semantic function of the Lord's Prayer, but also gives a vantage point for constructing the identity politics for the community of Matthew in the late first century CE. This is discussed in chapter 5.

---

19. Drake, "Did Jesus Oppose the *Prosbul*?," 241.

CHAPTER 2

A SOCIO-RHETORICAL ANALYTIC THEORY

THE GOAL OF THIS chapter is to present the tenets of a Socio-rhetorical Analytic Theory (SRAT) which is derived from blending some aspects of Vernon K. Robbins's Socio-rhetorical Interpretation (SRI) with social scientific concepts, particularly ideology and identity politics. The value of this blending is that not only are the resultants tenets of SRAT allowing one to explore principles for accomplishing literary analysis of a given text on account of Robbins's SRI, but also given the perspectives of ideology and identity politics, SRAT empowers the interpreter to explore principles for determining group relations reflected from the text. Briefly explored in this chapter are the tenets of SRAT in reference to Robbins's SRI, ideology and identity politics.

2.1 Vernon K. Robbins's Socio-Rhetorical Interpretation

In developing his Socio-rhetorical Interpretation (SRI), Robbins employs various categories from the social sciences, particularly anthropology and sociology, alongside linguistic perspectives to interpret the discourse of early Christian communities. Robbins's approach bears in mind both *emic* and *etic* sociological perspectives of interpretation. Thus, in pursuit of developing his SRI interpretative analytic framework, Robbins discusses the discourse of the early Christians considering a modern world view (the world outside the Biblical text). That is; the *etic* perspective, a reference to the world view outside the first century Mediterranean social setting and, the *emic* perspective, which is the cultural systems and institutions, and the world view of Antiquity, which is the world view of the Jesus movement (the world of the text). It is noteworthy that Robbins's SRI is a collection of essays, four by Robbins and three by Mack. Only the conclusion was jointly co-authored with Burton L. Mack.[1] Robbins also draws some perspective of his SRI from research works by Wayne A. Meeks[2] and John G. Gager.[3] In his SRI, Robbins adapts Bryan Wilson's seven types of religious sects, which are based on his findings from empirical sociological research.[4]

Robbins defines Socio-rhetorical Interpretation (SRI) as "an approach [not method] to literature that focuses on values, conviction, and beliefs both in the text we read and in the world we live." Thus, to Robbins, SRI "views [Biblical] text as performances of language in particular historical and cultural situations" which involves a multi-dimensional approach to textual analysis guided by a multi-dimensional hermeneutic.[5] Consequently, Robbins's SRI, which he has been developing over a period from 1984 to 2009 in pursuit of its analytical task, incorporates some aspects of certain social sciences theories such as rhetorical, social psychological and anthropological perspectives.[6] Robbins's SRI is primarily constituted of inner texture and inter texture.

Robbins refers to inner texture as a process of deriving the significance of a Biblical passage by observing the literary characteristics of peculiar words or phrases in a given passage by taking note of literary performances of the following textures of the words and phrases in the same passage; repetitive-progressive, opening-middle-closing, narrational, among other

---

1. Mack and Robbins, *Patterns of Persuasion*, discuss cultural categories which they referred to as "Typology of cultures" classified into five further categories: dominant culture, subculture, counterculture, contra-culture, and liminal culture.

2. Meeks, "The Man from Heaven," integrates both anthropological and sociological insights in order to rhetorically analyze the special patterns of language in the Gospel of John regarding the logic of the myth of the descending man and ascending redeemer. His analysis played a significant role in informing Robbins's social and cultural texture of a text in a manner that focuses on the inner texture of the text. Robbins, *Tapestry*, 144–45.

3. Gager, *Kingdom and Community*, employs twentieth century anthropological and sociological models to the study of early Christianity. These influenced Robbins's strategies for socio-rhetorical criticism. Robbins, *Tapestry*, 146–47.

4. Wilson, "Sect Development," 4–11, begins by differentiating a sect from a denomination. He further demonstrates how the genesis of sects is mostly associated with tensions within a religious body. His outline of seven types of sects: conversionist, revolutionist, intro-versionist, gnostic manipulation, thaumaturgical, reformist, and utopian, provides the basis for Robbins's specific social topics in religious literature to explain the early church's responses to the world. Robbins, *Tapestry*, 147–50.

5. Robbins, *Invention*, xxviii.

6. Robbins, "Socio-rhetorical Interpretation," discusses the conception of SRI and the development of his Socio-rhetorical Analytic from 1984 to 2009.

textures. Thus, through inner-textual analysis, an interpreter attempts to discover the inner voice of the passage from the literary function of peculiar words and phrases in that passage.[7]

Robbins's inter texture refers to a process of determining the significance of a passage by observing the relation between a Biblical text with an appropriate phenomenon outside the text in the light of an oral-scribal inter texture, the cultural inter texture, social inter texture and historical events outside that text.[8] By implication, Robbins's inter texture provides a literary witness to biblical texts because the approach attempts to find the meaning of a Biblical text by listening to the text's inner voice in relation to those emerging from other surrounding literary traditions outside the text. That is, from the literary traditions of a society contemporaneous to that text.

Because in Robbins socio-rhetorical interpretation the narrator plays a significant role in the task of interpreting a narrative, it is important to observe the relations between the author and the narrator in the task of interpretation. In the following diagram, Robbins displays a rhetorical axis of communication in inner texture which also shows the position of the author, implied author, narrator, and implied reader, real reader/audience:[9]

Real Author 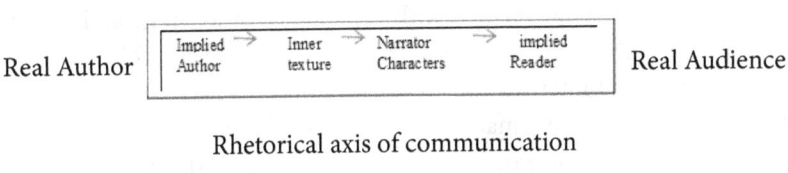 Real Audience

Rhetorical axis of communication

Using this diagram, Robbins demonstrates the various literary players that inform the meaning and significance of a text. From the diagram, it is clearly indicated that it is hardly possible to access the real author and real audience of the text from the text alone, because they stand outside the text. We also note from Robbins's rhetorical axis of communication that the real author, the narrator, and the implied author are differentiated by their relationship to the text. While the real author stands outside the text, the implied author stands inside of it. This means that while the implied author can be reconstructed from a text, the real author may not be fully accessed

7. Robbins, *Exploring*, 7–20; Robbins, *Tapestry*, 46–53.
8. Robbins, *Tapestry*, 96–143.
9. Robbins, *Tapestry*, 29.

from it, which is often problematic for two reasons. One, the readers of a text can only subjectively attempt to access the real author from the text. Two, how do we know the author's intention? It is through reading the text and then using it that we attempt to determine the author's intention, but this is often problematic because naturally text interpreters cannot always agree on an author's intention.

The authors' intentions in the New Testament are only knowable through the text, since we have no other access to them. Often, an author's intention turns out to be ambiguous. Therefore, Robbins's SRI favors rhetorical/literary interpretations that do not rely on an author's intentions but draw meaning in terms of the text's relationship with its social, economic and political environment. Consequently, in the case of Matthew's Gospel, the implied author and the narrator may be treated as one and the same because Matthew's implied author employs a narrative of Jesus as the main character and a plot that focuses on the emergence of Jesus, other characters (such as his disciples, his followers or the crowd), his work, death and ascension.

In this study, I limit my SRI borrowing to some of Robbins's inner texture and inter texture, leaving out his social and cultural textures because these have been supplemented with the models of ideology and identity politics highlighted in the next section of this chapter. While Robbins's inner texture and inter texture are useful in providing analytic principles that are relevant in the semantic analysis of Matthew's version of the Lord's Prayer or any Biblical text, ideology and identity politics supplement the inner texture and inter texture by providing analytic principles for describing group-relations of the community of Matthew in reference to other communities during their emergence in the late first century CE because New Testament scholars have observed that given the role of society in identity formation, we express who we are in reference to other people's group in our social environment.[10] This means, unlike biological identity, social identity formation is a relational enterprise.

2.2 Ideological Analysis

The understanding of ideology in this book is mainly grounded in the perspectives of ideology proposed by Eagleton, Robbins, Thomson, and

---

10. Esler, *The First Christians*, 28; M'bwangi, "Paul and Identity Construction," 4; Wanamaker, "Apocalypticism," 4.

Wanamaker. Eagleton defines ideology as "the way in which what we say and believe connects with the power-structures and the power-relations of the society we live in . . . those modes of feelings, valuing, perceiving and believing which have some kind of relations to the maintenance of social power."[11] In his definition, Eagleton presents two categories of social phenomena that inform the significance of the concept of ideology. They are: power-relations and power-structures that collectively link ideology to social domination.

The close link between ideology with domination or power to control has been observed by Thompson in the context of symbolic function. Thompson understands ideology as

> the ways in which the meaning mobilized by symbolic forms serves to establish and sustain relations of domination: to establish, in the sense that meaning may actively create and institute relations of domination; to sustain in the sense that meaning may serve to maintain and reproduce relations of domination through ongoing processes of producing and receiving symbolic forms.[12]

Besides a close link to power, domination and symbolism, ideology relates to speech and action. Grounding his definition in Eagleton, Robbins defines ideology as a reference to "the particular ways in which our speech and action in their social and cultural location, relate to and interconnect with resources, structures and institutions of power."[13] Robbins's definition adds two additional categories that are helpful in explaining the significance of ideology as a demonstration of power (whether socially or culturally located), namely; speech and action. Hence, the emphasis on terminology 'rhetoric' by Robbins in his SRI. Furthermore, because Robbins's understanding of ideology suggests that the maintenance and reproduction of social power are placed in the interest of "some but not others," Wanamaker rightly observed that in this case Robbins's perspective on ideology seems to imply a critical understanding of ideology, not a neutral one. Wanamaker's view is based on the suggestion that Robbins's stand for critical ideology is based on his use of Eagleton, who stands in the critical tradition of ideology.[14] Besides dominion, speech and action, Wanamaker links ideology to a process of legitimation.

11. Eagleton, *Literary Theory*, 15.
12. Thompson, *Revelation*, 56–57.
13. Robbins, *Tapestry*, 36.
14. Wanamaker, "'By the Power of God,'" 200–201.

Basing his views on Thompson, Wanamaker argues that as an analytical tool, ideological analysis attends to four tasks: first is the crucial study of symbolic forms of social meanings. Second, to examine the social context in which symbolic forms are used. Third is to explore the ways in which the meanings generated by symbolic forms can be used to produce and maintain relations of dominion. The fourth task of ideological analysis is to identify the general modes in which ideology operates. For instance; the two ways of justifying legitimation. On the one hand, ideological analysis explores legitimation through "rationalization." That is, the application of "interconnected reasons" to rationalize or defend social institutions, or social relations. On the other hand, exploring the legitimation process in ideological analysis requires one to investigate how legitimation is justified through "universalization" by portraying features of the institute that in reality serve the interests of a few people, while claiming to serve the interests of everybody, to justify legitimation.[15]

Furthermore, Max Weber and Peter Berger's theories supplement Wanamaker's notion of the process by which legitimation takes place through traditionalizing of sacred references. On the one hand, Weber noted that adherents of charismatic movements tend to either traditionalize or rationalize the status of a movement in order to legitimate their charismatic authority (Weber 1968, 246). On the other hand, Berger contends that some leaders tend to legitimate the beliefs of a movement through a sacred frame of reference to bestow ontological (nature of being) status to the movement and facilitate its validity and sustenance in a manner that transcends its own history.[16]

Given the above brief discussion, in this study ideology refers to *a mindset derived from the use of speech, action or/and artifacts to symbolize power generated either to sustain or to oppose structures of domination for the purpose of negotiate identity in the society.*

This definition of ideology, derived from Robbins, Wanamaker, and Berger, portrays analytical principles relevant in revealing power relations embedded in Matthew's version of the Lord's Prayer that can only be envisioned by exploring significance of the symbols of power relations and power structures emerging from the Roman Empire, the Jesus Movement (Early Christian communities), and Diaspora Judaism, and how these relations impacted the conception of the cultural identity of the Matthean

---

15. Wanamaker, "'By the Power of God,'" 200–201.
16. Berger, *Sacred Canopy*, 33–34.

community from the point of view of Matthew's narrative in his version of the Lord's Prayer. This conception of the analytical task of critical ideology calls for certain concepts that signify certain political, religious, and cultural structures associated with identity formation in Antiquity, such as ethnicity, deity, geography, taxation, baptism, family, and law. These concepts will be explored to elaborate on the social context which triggered Matthew to compose his Gospel with hermeneutical focus on the concept of righteousness. Thus, in Matthew's Gospel, "righteousness" stands as a kind of ideology for shaping the identity of his community. This is elaborated in chapter five by observing the relationship between righteousness with other concepts such as Πάτερ ἡμῶν (our Father), βασιλεία (Kingdom) and, ἄρτος (bread) found in the Lord's Prayer in Matthew 6:19–23. To this end, we turn to the contribution of identity politics, a crucial constituent element of the Socio-rhetorical Analytic Theory (SRAT).

2.3 Identity Politics Analysis

Having outlined the rationale for Robbins socio-rhetorical interpretation and ideology in the socio-rhetorical analytic theory, it is time to set out the definition of identity politics to describe its contribution in this theoretical model. Before we define the identity politics, it is crucial to answer this question: in the face of first century CE group interaction, how did individuals and groups negotiate their identity in society? In reference to social identity theory, recategorization, identification and comparison help us to describe how identity was negotiated in Antiquity. First, recategorization refers to the division of the social world into assessable group entities, whose main three preconditions are depersonalization, stereotyping, and vilification.[17] This is pertinent for elaborating the dynamics of group relations in identity formation. In pursuit of this, depersonalization, stereotyping, and vilification are vital preconditions to recategorization because they collectively facilitate peoples' self-conceptions of who they are in terms of community membership, and in the less favorable attitudes towards the outer group.[18] Stereotype refers to a conception of peoples' self-awareness of who they are in terms of their group membership, rather than unique individual traits. Stereotypical categories may bear

---

17. Esler, "Group Norms," 164–65; Faulkner, "Jewish Identity," 3–4; Kuecker, "Ethnicity and Social Identity," 70.
18. Faulkner, "Jewish Identity," 2–4; Kuecker, "Ethnicity and Social Identity," 70.

either negative or positive connotations.[19] Vilification, like stereotypes, conceives identity in terms of group membership, but mostly appeals to derogatory language or prejudice against members of an outer group.[20] To address the negative effects of vilification and stereotyping that tend to perpetuate inter-group hostility and antagonism, recategorization into a superordinate category is necessary. A superordinate category refers to the redrawing of group boundaries in order to bring into one group members of an in-group and out-group, without collapsing their distinctiveness, but in a manner that acknowledges their commonality.[21]

Second, 'identification,' which refers to the notion of human beings' preference to belong to a group because they conceive it to rightfully express a self-conception of who they are, is usually coupled with recategorization to procure identity. The precondition for identification is the existence of two or more individuals who conceive themselves as members of a group.[22] Belonging to a group is driven by two factors, namely; (1) a desire to maintain self-esteem and (2) to have their life guided by group norms. In some cases, identification, such as in ethnic groupings, presents rigid boundaries of identity, unlike in such a case as belonging to a football club.[23] Third, besides recategorization and identification, identity was negotiated through 'comparison' and 'accommodation.' On the one hand, comparison refers to the maintenance of one's awareness of who they are through a process of observing similarities and differences, by which groups favorably differentiate themselves. Because comparison is applied positively as a mode of expression of in-group self-love rather than out-group hatred, comparison generally aims to maintain the positive social identity of a group. For example, economic status, purity codes, or language may have been used to refer to one group in comparison to a higher status group in order to boost the in-group's identity against an "outer group."[24] On the other hand, accommodation which refers to merging of cultural traditions whereby some cultural traditions are subordinated to the other for the purposes of

---

19. Esler, *Conflict and Identity*, 21–22; Kuecker, "Ethnicity and Social Identity," 70.
20. Faulkner, "Jewish Identity," 3–4.
21. Baker, "Narrative-Identity Model," 107–8.
22. Faulkner, "Jewish Identity," 3–4.
23. Faulkner, "Jewish Identity," 2–3; Kuecker, "Ethnicity and Social Identity," 70–71.
24. Kuecker, "Ethnicity and Social Identity," 71–72.

reinterpretation,[25] points to Matthew's use of Judean traditions, for instance Kaddish and Shimoneh Esreh to negotiate the identity of his community.

Given the function of recategorization, identification and comparison in Antiquity, identity was not focused on self-individuation. Rather, the individual was understood and expressed in relation to others. Malina and Neyrey in *Portraits of Paul: An Archeology of Ancient Personality*, claim that in Antiquity,

> the most elementary unit of social analysis is not the individual person considered apart from others as a unique being. Rather, it is the collectivist person, the group-embedded person, the person always in relation with and connected to at least one other social unit, usually a kinship group.[26]

Thus, in Antiquity, the individual was known not from his personal preference but on account of the group's norms and aspirations. Thus, Malina and Neyrey apply the concept of embeddedness, which refers to "a social-psychological quality describing the dimensions of group-oriented persons by which all members of the group share a common perspective."[27] This dyadic personality, that is; the expression and the knowledge of the individual through other people or institutions, is confirmed by Plutarch (c. 46–120 CE), a Greek biographer and essayist, who later became a Roman citizen, in his *Dialogue on Love* when he claimed that "The nurses rule the infant, the teacher the boy, the gymnasiarch the youth, his admirer the Youngman who, when he comes of age, is ruled by law and his commanding general. No one is his own master, no one is unrestricted."[28]

If we understand Plutarch's "rule" to be explicitly pointing to the expression of knowledge, then the above passage confirms that a person's identity was expressed in relation to the mentor or associations to which one belonged. Malina and Neyrey observe that expressions of identity, as rhetorically expressed by Plutarch, indicate that in Antiquity, "persons . . . define themselves almost exclusively in terms of the groups in which they are embedded. Their total self-awareness emphatically depends on such group embeddedness."[29] Thus, in Antiquity, group norms, rather than individual or self-choice and decisions, such as those in a household,

25. Barclay, *Jews in the Mediterranean Diaspora*, 96.
26. Malina and Neyrey, *Portraits of Paul*, 157.
27. Malina and Neyrey, *Portraits of Paul*, 159.
28. Plutarch, *Dialogue* 338–39.
29. Malina and Neyrey, *Portraits of Paul*, 158.

kinship, family, clan, factions, or cultic associations, provided modes of identity formation, as shall be discussed in relation to the cultural identity formation in the Roman Empire, Diaspora Judaism, the Jesus Movement and the Matthean community.

If recategorization, identification, comparison, accommodation and dyadic personality describe the process of negotiating identity in the Antiquity, then how do we define "identity politics"? Sylvia Tesh and Bruce Williams view identity politics as "the demand based on lived experiences of common knowledge and shared values of ordinary people evident in women's, gay and lesbian and civil rights movements, where members struggle to replace negative stereotypes with robust and positive images of themselves."[30] Even though Tesh and Williams in their definition have not specified the point of reference from which the collective action is determined, they present the subjects of identity politics as aggravated persons contesting together to defend their collective self-esteem. Mary Bernstein's perception of identity politics as "the emergency of a way to make sense of, engage and change the social condition of stigmatization and material disadvantaged people" portrays identity politics as a social movement that intends to mitigate social malevolence.[31] Unfortunately, Bernstein has left out the subject of her version of identity politics, that is; she does not describe the "actors" of this perspective of identity politics.

In defining identity politics as "narratives of collective selfhood . . . that help to guide people's actions and simultaneously constitute individuals and collectivities" as they attempt to answer the question of "who are we (consciousness), how we define others (boundaries), what is the source of our problem, and how we can make the world better (politics)," Dawn Moon presents a definition of identity politics that focuses on the function of the individual self ("I") and collective selfhood ("we") in forming and maintaining the function of a social movement.[32] Moon's definition of identity politics is more plausible than that proposed by either Tesh, Williams, or Bernstein because it goes beyond perceiving identity politics as merely a social movement by regarding the concept 'identity politics' as a 'result' of collective and individual narratives.

However, the expression of identity in reference to dyadic personality which puts more emphasis on group-embeddedness rather

---

30. Tesh and Williams, "Identity Politics," 294.
31. Tesh and Williams, "Identity Politics," 294; Bernstein, "Identity Politics."
32. Moone, "Who Am I?," 1340.

individual psychological self-perception, challenges modern theories of identity politics, particularly, Moon's identity politics. The main challenge is Moon's conception of her understanding that in modern identity politics, identity is expressed in collective selfhood. The concept of collective selfhood would have been a strange, if not anachronistic way of conceiving expressions of identity in Antiquity, because in ancient times identity was often expressed via group-embeddedness rather than collective selfhood. Applying Moon's psychological self-decision-making concept would be anachronistic with respect to Antiquity because at that time, the identity of the individual was based on dyadic personality. That is, individual identity was derived from belonging to a collective of some sort or in relation to other people or cities.

In addition, exploring Dawn Moon's perspective of social evangelistic movement mode of identity politics is crucial because in chapter 5 it provides the tenets for guiding in achieving the goal of identity politics envisioned in this book. Moon defines the social movement evangelism mode as any process of teaching others that "there is good and evil, and recruiting them to the side of good."[33] Moon, exemplifying the function of a social evangelism mode of identity politics, says that "a group may, for instance, see the teachings of Mao or Trotsky as the truth that redeems people from the evils of capitalism and defines outsiders as those lost to the truth."[34] Moon's social movement evangelism mode of identity politics entails deliverance from ignorance and subjection to social injustices described as "evils." Thus, Moon contends that the goal of social movement evangelism is "to transform individuals [by] creating redeemed selves" in the process.[35] What is the *modus operandi* of social movement evangelism?

To execute its operations, the social movement evangelism mode of identity politics focuses on "its combination of a consciousness of the self as fluid, and a focus on the individual level of transformation."[36] In this case, Moon affirms a three-fold process through which the operations of the social movement evangelism mode are accomplished: (1) the conception of the self as fluid allows transformation to take place on account of psychological self-decision making; (2) Manichaean boundaries emphasize rigidity made possible by the conception of reality in terms

---

33. Moone, "Who Am I?," 1363.
34. Moone, "Who Am I?," 1363.
35. Moone, "Who Am I?," 1363.
36. Moone, "Who Am I?," 1363.

of the contrast between good and evil and; (3) a focus on the individual implies that transformation is to be understood as the redemption of the individual as opposed to a group.

Given the processes of negotiating identity and the definition of identity politics explored so far, we should now be able to define 'identity politics' that befits the discussion of group-relations of the community of Matthew in the late first century CE. From the definitions and the process of negotiating identity so far explored, the following concepts offer the appropriate nuances for the definition of identity politics which will be used in this monograph: power struggles, group and individual narratives, group image, disenfranchised community, values/beliefs. For the purposes of this study, I define identity politics as the *borrowing and accommodation of beliefs, values and norms of an ancient traditional community by a marginal group to reconstruct their identity through recategorization, identification and contestation in order to overcome domination by a majority group and achieve the goal of encouraging non-violent attitude, advocate social good and promote an inclusive household.* This definition of identity politics and the other one for ideology already explored will work hand in hand with a modified view of Dawn Moon's social evangelistic mode of identity politics to describe how Matthew uses his version of the Lord's Prayer to construct the identity politics for his community.

2.4 Conclusion

The above analysis presents the Socio-rhetorical Analysis Theory. This theory presents interpretative principles that are crucial in describing Matthew's version of the Lord's Prayer as the author's ideology conveyed by the symbolism, speech, and actions of both the figure of Jesus and the implied author reflected in the text as a means to expound the significance of greater righteousness (Matt 5:20), contrasted by the public display of the hypocrites but symbolized by the prayer done in secret and in trusting God (6:5–7) and in an attitude similar to that of alms giving (6:5–7). This conception of ideology prompts the question: how did Matthew employ his version of the Lord's Prayer to procure Christian identity for his community in the first century social setting? To appropriately apply Moon's theory of identity politics to explain the reconstruction and legitimation of a first-century Christian identity from the Lord's Prayer in Matthew 6:9–13, as it will be elaborated in chapter five, social evangelistic and contestive-accommodation mode of identity politics is premised on the principle that marginal groups may accommodate group beliefs, values and norms of a traditional group to contest against a dominating group in order to redeem unredeemed individuals. To this end, semantic analysis of the Lord's Prayer using a socio-rhetorical interpretation is crucial before exploring the social setting of the community of Matthew in the first century CE.

CHAPTER 3

SEMANTIC ANALYSIS OF MATTHEW 6:9–13

ROBBINS'S INNER TEXTURE AND intertexture categories of socio-rhetorical interpretation in this chapter are useful in helping us to discern the *emic* rhetorical significance conveyed by Matthew's version of the Lord's Prayer in terms of internal and external voices, respectively, of the first century CE.

3.1 Inner Textual Analysis

3.1.1 Repetitive-Progressive Inner Texture

The repetitive-progressive texture communicates meaning and effects which reformulate the meaning and function through the repetition of verbs and nouns, which produce patterns and concepts within the literary structure, semantic functions, and content of a passage. To emphasize the effectiveness of rhetoric in the process of progression, the interpreter stresses (1) the relations between "signs and sounds rather than content and meaning" and (2) may use a diagram to plot the repeated words and phrases in a vertical column which list characters and concepts in the discourse.[1] What is the value of carefully observing repetitive-progressive patterns in Biblical scholarship? The value of observing repetitive-progressive patterns lays in the fact that the inner linguistic features of verbs, concepts, nouns, etc. present relations which are significant in understanding the nature of the discourse of the early Christians behind the Biblical text.[2] Robbins suggests some guiding questions that can help in accomplishing the task of observing repetitive-progressive patterns:

1. Robbins, *Exploring*, 9–14; Robbins, *Tapestry*, 47–49.
2. Robbins, *Tapestry*, 49.

SEMANTIC ANALYSIS OF MATTHEW 6:9–13

What patterns emerge from the repetition of particular topics in the text? What topics replace the other topics in the progression of the text? Is the repetition a continuous one or are there some interruptions or modifications observable? Do the repetitions tend to gather together or separate some words? Are there any repetitions that create a context for a new word in the progression?[3]

The repetitive-progressive inner texture can be observed by taking note of the Greek text of Matt 6:9–13 (NA28). The next step is to observe the textual significance of Matthew's version of the Lord's Prayer in the SM by examining the repetitive-progressive inner texture. The following sentence diagram will guide this semantic analysis.

```
9   οὖν προσεύχεσθε ὑμεῖς            orientation
        Οὕτως
            Πάτερ                     familial/communal/household
                ἡμῶν
                ὁ ἐν τοῖς οὐρανοῖς,   transcendent sphere
                ἁγιασθήτω   τὸ ὄνομά  general action on earth
                            σου.
10          Ἐλθέτω      ἡ βασιλεία
                        σου.
            Γενηθήτω τὸ θέλημά τῆς γῆς.   comparision in manner
                        σου,    ἐπὶ
                        ὡς
                        οὐρανῷ
                        ἐν
            καὶ                           introducing specific action
11          δὸς     Τὸν ἄρτον   ἡμῖν
            σήμερον     ἡμῶν
                        τὸν ἐπιούσιον
12          Καὶ
            ἄφες  τὰ ὀφειλήματα  ἡμῖν
                        ἡμῶν,
                ὡς καὶ
                ἡμεῖς  ἀφίεμεν  ὀφειλέταις
                                    τοῖς
```

---

3. Robbins, *Tapestry*, 50.

THE LORD'S PRAYER IN MATTHEW 6:9-13

         ἡμῶν.

13 Καὶ   introducing dependence
 εἰσενέγκῃς ἡμᾶς πειρασμόν,
   μὴ   εἰς
 ἀλλὰ
  ῥῦσαι ἡμᾶς πονηροῦ
       ἀπὸ τοῦ.

  In this prayer, some nouns are repeatedly mentioned at different points. For instance, οὐρανός (heaven) is mentioned twice (vv. 9 and 10) as the abode of God and the realm where 'God's will' is operational, respectively. It is noteworthy that the first heaven is in the plural form, while the second is singular. Although βασιλεία (kingdom) appears only once (v. 10a) in this prayer, it is conspicuously set semantically to connect the petition for God's name to be sanctified (v. 9) and his will to be done (v. 10b). Elsewhere in the SM βασιλεία (kingdom) is associated with suffering for righteousness' sake (5:10), with prioritizing (6:33), and with discourse of the parables of the kingdom (13:1-35). Moreover, in the Matthean Lord's Prayer, two nouns—ὀφείλημα and ὀφειλέτης—with similar meaning because they originate from the same root, are also mentioned. In these two nouns, one refers to the abstract notion of "debt" or "obligations," hence the neuter plural τὰ ὀφειλήματα (debts), and the other to personal ones τοῖς ὀφειλέταις (debtors), hence the masculine. Similarly, the first-person plural pronoun ἡμῶν (our) is mentioned four times (vv. 9, 11, 12) to express a familial or communal perspective of God, communal bread-provision, and communal debt/sins/offense. Thus, the repetitive pattern reveals a communal nature of the prayer. Noteworthy is the presence of the negative particle μὴ (not) in 6:13 which modifies εἰσενέγκῃς (bring into, cause).

  Given the above sentence flow, the repetitive-progressive inner texture allows us to observe the thematic discussions concerning righteousness, God's household, and human obligations from the Lord's Prayer. Firstly, because the Lord's Prayer is introduced in 6:1 by a warning which prohibits the followers of Jesus from practicing (μὴ ποιεῖν) their righteousness in order to seek public honor (to be seen by people), it indicates that the reciting of the Lord's Prayer, like practicing and teaching of Jesus's commands (5:19) is an act of righteousness that can be classified as surpassing that of the teachers of the law and the Pharisees (Matt 5:20). Some progression is observable in this prayer. Here we see some repetitive-progressive inner texture which overlaps with Jesus's saying on the law (5:17–20), and his saying about the introduction to the Lord's Prayer (6:1). While righteousness in 5:20 declares in a general sense the condition for entering the kingdom of heaven, in 6:1 a particular action is introduced that provides the content for both verses (5:19, 20). Consequently, righteousness is crucial to the progression of thought; it introduces a general condition which is elaborated by the introduction of a particular action the (prayer that does not seek honor from the public) which in turn prepares the grounds for the Lord's Prayer (6:9-13).

Second, it is noted above that the Matthean Lord's Prayer has seven imperative verbs that relate to entreating God. The act of praying refers to God as ἡμῶν Πάτερ (our Father), on account of this prayer being taught by Jesus to his disciples. It is very possible that ἡμῶν Πάτερ is grounded in the Jewish conception of God, particularly on account of Betz's suggestion that the Matthean Lord's Prayer belongs to liturgical material containing the type of prayer which, "derives, when it is written down, from oral tradition."[4] Jeremias argued that since, in Palestinian Judaism, God was understood to be unique, to address God either as "Abba," or "our Father" would have been disrespectful, although Jesus used it in order to express a special relationship with God.[5] Following Jeremias, Kittel contends that referring to God as Πάτερ (Father) would have sounded familiar, but disrespectful to Jesus's contemporaries, because although אבי (abba) was used in Jewish religious speech, it had to be accompanied by an addition to emphasize distance between man and God such as "who is in heaven."[6] Davies and Allison, contrary to Jeremias and Kittel, say that the concept of "[our Father] is quite easily explained as being influenced by the Jewish liturgy," because it is found in Shimoneh Esreh's petition 4 and 6 and in Mishnah, *M. Sota* 9.15 and *Yoma* 8.9, as well in the Gospel of Mark 14:36.[7] The debate on the problem of the influence of Judaism on ἡμῶν Πάτερ (our Father) does not begin and end with Jeremias, Davies, and Allison, but continues with other scholars such as Géza Vermès.[8] A reference to God whose abode is ἐν τοῖς οὐρανοῖς (in the heavens), on account of the semantic function of

---

4. Betz, *Sermon on the Mount*, 370.
5. Jeremias, *Prayers of Jesus*, 29–57, 62.
6. *TDOT* 5.
7. Davies and Allison, *Saint Matthew*, 600.
8. See Vermès's two volumes: *Jesus the Jew*, 210–11; *Jesus and the World of Judaism*, 39–43.

the expression ἡμῶν Πάτερ implies that the petitioner belongs to a family of the transcendent God who is also immanent since τὸ θέλημά σου, ὡς ἐν οὐρανῷ καὶ ἐπὶ γῆς (let your will be done, upon the earth as also in heaven) indicates that God's will is requested for the earth in a similar fashion to the heavens. This also alludes to an eschatological immanence.

Thirdly, the imperative ἄφες and the noun ὀφειλέταις in Matthew 6:12, which can be translated as "forgive" and "debtor," respectively,[9] is probably used here metaphorically to stress the importance of reciprocity in forgiveness as a means of fostering human relationships. The Lord's Prayer shows some repetitive-progressive inner texture in the context of entreating God to act on earth. The repetitive mentioning of ἐν οὐρανῷ in 6:10 in the context of the imperatives ἁγιασθήτω (sanctify), ἐλθέτω (let come) and, γενηθήτω (let be done) in verses 9 and 10 entreats God to act in a general way on earth in a similar measure as in heaven. Verses 11–13 employ imperatives δὸς (give), ἄφες (forgive, pardon), and ῥῦσαι (recue, deliver) and the subjunctive εἰσενέγκῃς (lead into, cause) to entreat God to act by making specific provisions. The personal pronoun ἐγώ (verb-tobe: Iam), is mentioned six times in the plural, that is; each case twice in the dative, possessive, and accusative which describe the object of God's action on Earth. Finally, this progression moves from entreating God to act generally, act specifically and culminates in a declaration Ἀμήν, which according to BDAG, declares the affirmation, "let it be so."[10] How does the opening-middle-closing contribute to the inner voice of the text?

3.1.2 Opening-Middle-Closing Inner Texture

Robbins's open-middle-closing pattern helps us to explore a threefold literary structural content of the Lord's Prayer in Matthew 6:9–13. While the repetitive-progressive pattern emerges from word analysis, the opening- middle-closing texture is a product of the exploration of the repetitive-progressive pattern. How does the opening, middle and closing of a text aid the task of analyzing inner-texture, and what is its main goal? According to Robbins, to achieve the goals of the opening-middle-closing aspect of analysis, it is important for interpreters to do the following:[11] (1) correlate their sub-units with the overall unit to explain their rhetorical function in

9. BDAG 156, 742.
10. BDAG 53.
11. Robbins, *Exploring*, 19–20; Robbins, *Tapestry*, 51–52.

SEMANTIC ANALYSIS OF MATTHEW 6:9-13

relation to each other, and (2) bear in mind that the goal of opening-middle-closing analysis is to discern the persuasive effects of the various parts, and how they work together in relation to the persuasive nature of the text. The following are some of the critical questions noted by Robbins that guide the task of achieving the goal of opening-middle-closing aspects:

> (1) what is the nature of the opening of a unit [or passage] in relation to closure? What is the nature of the topics at the beginning in relation to the topics at the end of a unit? (2) What is the nature of the topics that replace the topics at the beginning? (3) Is there repetition connecting the beginning, middle and end? Or (4) is the repetition limited only to a particular section of the texture? (5) What is the function of the parts of texts in relation to the whole passage?[12]

The value of opening-middle-closing analysis in socio-rhetorical interpretation lies in preparing the interpreter for detailed analysis of the narrational and argumentative texture.

At its opening, the Lord's Prayer is marked by the inferential conjunction οὖν (then, accordingly) which indicates that what follows is an inference from the second clause in 6:8, which in turn points back to 6:1. Thus, Matthew's narrative presents the Lord's Prayer as an extension of Jesus's discussion in 6:1-8. Additionally, the opening of this prayer is further modified by the adverb Οὕτως (thus) preceding the inferential particle οὖν, marking a conclusion, and the future imperative verb προσεύχεσθε (prostrate, pray). Therefore, this introduction in the Matthean Lord's Prayer should be translated, 'Therefore pray in this manner.' Two crucial semantic functions of this introduction to Lord's Prayer are notable. First, in the section prior to the Lord's Prayer (Matt 6:7-8) Nolland observes that it "displays a relaxed confidence about God's prior knowledge and his fatherly commitment."[13] In contrast, Betz claims that it involves a chiastic "argument begun with the critique of wrong performance (vs 7a) and wrong theory (vs 7b), in order then to turn to correct theory (vs 8), and now to the correct practice (vs 9a), exemplified by the Lord's Prayer (vs 9b-13)."[14] Second, Betz says that in the context of the stated chiasm, the conjunction οὖν (thus) "serves as affirmation of the theology of vss 7-8."[15] Thus, in this opening part of the Lord's

---

12. Robbins, *Tapestry*, 53.
13. Nolland, *Gospel of Matthew*, 285.
14. Betz, *Sermon on the Mount*, 369.
15. Betz, *Sermon on the Mount*, 369.

Prayer, Jesus is presented as one who orients his disciples towards right way of practicing a group or communal prayer.

The middle of the prayer is divided into two. The section covered by verses 9b–10b has God as its focus in reference to evoking God's name to be sanctified; His kingdom and will to come into being. These two petitions which collectively constitute the middle of the prayer are related to each other. This petition invoking ἐλθέτω ἡ βασιλεία σου (let your kingdom come), standing in the middle, ties the three petitions together and its semantic significance has provoked a debate among scholars. For instance, while Guelich asserts that this phrase indicates, "when God establishes his sovereignty, revealing himself as the holy one of Israel, his purposes and will among his people and his own earth are accomplished,"[16] Betz argues that the phrase refers to the eschatological arrival of the kingdom of God, and its complete victory over evil.[17] Nolland, advancing Betz's eschatological aspect, says that the phrase ἐλθέτω ἡ βασιλεία σου creates expectancy by pointing out that, "the kingdom of God was not only being announced as imminent by Jesus . . . but also that Jesus's own ministry represented the present stirrings of the coming kingdom."[18] Matthew's narrative seems to employ Jesus's sayings on prayer regarding the kingdom of God to emphasize Jesus's eschatological role as the Messiah as one who himself is a manifestation of the nature of God's kingdom on earth. The second part of the middle is marked by verses 11, 12, and 13. These three verses focus on human need considering daily provisions, forgiveness and seeking empowerment to overcome evil. Keener tells us that the second part of the middle (vv. 11–13) expresses dependence on God for daily sustenance, promises God's grace commensurate with one's obedience in forgiving others, and pleads for God's protection in testing of one's faith in Jesus.[19]

The Closing part of Matthew's Lord's Prayer (Ὅτι σοῦ ἐστιν ἡ βασιλεία καὶ ἡ δύναμις καὶ ἡ δόξα εἰς τοὺς αἰῶνας. Ἀμήν: Matt 6:13b) is introduced in verse 13 by the conjunction Ὅτι (since, because) which stands like a benediction, and is absent in some older Greek manuscripts such as ℵ, B, D, Z and 0170, but is found in more recent manuscripts such as L, W, 0, 0233 and f13. The Matthean community must have used the section found in older manuscripts; the end of the Lord's Prayer for them may have been

---

16. Guelich, *Sermon on the Mount*, 311.
17. Betz, *Sermon on the Mount*, 390.
18. Nolland, *Gospel of Matthew*, 287.
19. Keener, *Gospel of Matthew*, 224.

stated thus: Καὶ μὴ εἰσενέγκῃς ἡμᾶς εἰς πειρασμόν, ἀλλὰ ῥῦσαι ἡμᾶς ἀπὸ τοῦ πονηροῦ (Matt 6:13a). Nolland has noted that this two-fold petition refers to two issues: one, πειρασμός (temptations) and πονηρός (evil) are conceptually related, "the first part envisages God bringing the person into certain situation, while the second has in mind a rescuing of a person out of situation."[20] Nolland's notion suggests that God puts people into temptation and then delivers them, an idea refuted by Betz. Grounding his argument on Job (1:12; 2:6; 42:25, 7–17), Betz says that "God himself does not carry out temptation, but he leaves it to Satan."[21] Similar to Betz's interpretation, Lamprecht regards the phrase μὴ εἰσενέγκῃς ἡμᾶς εἰς πειρασμόν (lead us not into temptation) in this sixth petition of the Lord's Prayer as indicative of "Yahweh's perfect plan for humanity," in which case temptation is to be understood as a means of God's wisdom by which he "leads his children to the destiny which he has appointed for them."[22] Given that εἰσφέρω means to "cause someone to enter into certain . . . condition,"[23] in view of Job's experiences stated by Betz, it seems this section of the Matthean Lord's prayer intends to emphasize the power of God in overcoming evil in comparison to the inability of humans to overcome evil in order to stress human beings' dependence on God.

From this opening-middle-closing literary structure, the progression of the prayer that begins under Jesus's instructions continues by focusing first on exalting God on earth, attending to human needs on earth, then ending with affirming God's sovereignty is apparent. Thus, the prayer has a chiasm with the phrase ὡς ἐν οὐρανῷ καὶ ἐπὶ γῆς (as in heaven also upon the earth) at its center in order to emphasize not only humankind's dependence on God but also to demonstrate the sovereignty of God over evil on earth:

v. 9   οὕτως οὖν προσεύχεσθε ὑμεῖς
      Πάτερ ἡμῶν ὁ ἐν τοῖς οὐρανοῖς·
        Ἁγιασθήτω τὸ ὄνομά σου·
          v10.ἐλθάτω ἡ βασιλεία σου·
        γενηθήτω τὸ θέλημά σου,
      ὡς ἐν οὐρανῷ καὶ ἐπὶ γῆς·

20. Nolland, *Gospel of Matthew*, 291.
21. Betz, *Sermon on the Mount*, 407.
22. Lamprecht, "Reading Matthew," 22.
23. BDAG 295.

v. 11	τόν ἄρτον ἡμῶν τὸν ἐπιούσιον δὸς ἡμῖν σήμερον
v. 12	καὶ ἄφες ἡμῖν τὰ ὀφειλήματα ἡμῶν,
	ὡς καὶ ἡμεῖς ἀφήκαμεν τοῖς ὀφειλέταις ἡμῶν
v. 13	καὶ μὴ εἰσενέγκῃς ἡμᾶς εἰς πειρασμόν,
	ἀλλὰ ῥῦσαι ἡμᾶς ἀπὸ τοῦ πονηροῦ

From this chiasmus, the reader should notice that the main emphasis in the prayer is to evoke God's action on earth in order to establish his sovereign rule in the same measure as in heaven. This is expressed in a chiastic style, first by invoking God to act generally on earth as expressed by three imperatives: Ἁγιασθήτω, ἐλθάτω, and γενηθήτω; second, in a C'B'A' characteristic, the prayer recognizes God's specific action on earth expressed by provision for bread (τόν ἄρτον ἡμῶν), forgiveness from debt/sin (ἄφες ἡμῖν τὰ ὀφειλήματα ἡμῶν), and deliverance from evil (μὴ εἰσενέγκῃς . . . ἀλλὰ ῥῦσαι ἡμᾶς). Thus, ὡς ἐν οὐρανῷ καὶ ἐπὶ γῆς (upon the earth as also in heaven) plays a significant role of sustaining the chiasmus. This prompts the question; why was the establishing of God's sovereign rule on earth important to the Matthean community? Or, could the Matthean community have felt somehow marginalized or disenfranchised to the point of relying on God's, rather than man's intervention? Chapter 5 provides the answer by examining the relations of the Matthean community with the Roman Empire, Diaspora Judaism and the Jesus Movement from the point of view of the rhetorical function of the Lord's Prayer. Having explored the opening-middle-closing texture, we turn to the narrational inner texture to continue listening to the inner voice of the text from Matthew's authorial contributions.

3.1.3 Narrational Inner Texture

The focus of this section is to use Robbins's inter texture to explore the narrative discourse of the Lord's Prayer as presented by Matthew, the implied author. The narrational texture is the analysis of a discourse from the point of view of the interpreter's focus on the narrator and characters. How is the analysis of narrational texture undertaken? It is noteworthy that early Christianity emerged in a "rhetorical culture." That is, a kind of culture that "is aware of written text, uses written text and oral language interactively" in which case written texts are viewed as additional tools that give power to language.[24] Socio-rhetorical interpretation attempts to avoid the literalist approach that focuses on "distinguishing between real author, implied author, narrator, characters, narratee, implied reader and real reader," whose main weakness, as Robbins observes, is to allow "literary critics to regularly re-enact the rhetoric of the narrator rather than exhibit the nature of that rhetoric to their readers."[25] To avoid this folly, socio-rhetorical interpretation regards the text as having the voice to speak for itself which calls for the analysis not to attempt to create real reader, real author, or real audience, but rather to reconstruct the implied author, speech, narrator and implied audience.[26] This is because primarily socio-rhetorical interpretation as rhetorical theory is grounded on "the presupposition that speaker, speech and audience are primary constituents of a situation of communication." Moreover, the contrasting arguments that may appeal to analogy or written testimony play a significant role in addressing the concerns of a narrational nature.[27] Thus, the approach of socio-rhetorical interpretation in narrational analysis sounds more realistic than literary theorists' that attempt to discover the real author, or real audience from a written text. In any case, if one happens to read a piece of literature from the inner texture perspective, the image of the author from the text is reconstructed according to one's perception of a text's literary dynamics.

The aim of narrational inner texture is to explore Matthew's narration of Jesus's story in the Lord's Prayer. Before proceeding, it is important to know how the Gospel of Matthew was composed, in order to be familiar with Matthew's development of his plot. Shirley Jackson Case tells us that Matthew wrote his Gospel to present the story of Jesus for "convenient form for ordinary use."[28] Outlining the constituents of Matthew's Gospel narrative, Case states, "a judicious selection of different types of material, Jesus's teachings arranged topically and distributed at regular intervals throughout the book, and a variety of subject-matter introduced, made a treatise particularly well adapted to meet the various needs."[29] Case implies that in writing the Lord's Prayer, Matthew as the implied author deliberately employed the story of Jesus to addresses a variety of cultural needs in his audience. To explore

---

24. Robbins, *Tapestry*, 56–57.
25. Robbins, *Tapestry*, 54–55.
26. Robbins, *Tapestry*, 15.
27. Robbins, *Tapestry*, 45.
28. Case, "Origin and Purpose," 391.
29. Case, "Origin and Purpose," 391.

how Matthew uses Jesus's story to address these needs, I shall focus on a narrational analysis of Matthew's Lord's Prayer (6:9-13).

The narrational inner texture of Matthew's Lord's Prayer presents the Matthean Jesus as the narrator of the prayer. Jesus introduces the prayer after warning them to "Beware of practicing your righteousness before men in order to be seen by them" (Matt 6:1). The shorter Lucan version of the Lord's Prayer has Jesus introducing the prayer to his disciples upon their request to Jesus, saying, "Lord teach us to pray as John taught his disciples" (Luke 11:1). If the Lord's Prayer in Matthew's Gospel narrative is viewed as a continuation of Jesus's warning on how not to practice acts of righteousness in public (6:1), then Matthew's Gospel presents the Lord's Prayer as an 'expression' or 'act' of righteousness acceptable to the standards set and proclaimed by Jesus himself. Thus, the teaching *chreia* in which the narrator attributes speech in the form of instructions to the disciples saying, "therefore pray like this" (Matt 6:9), characterizes Jesus as the one holding the power to authorize the prayer as an act of righteousness. The prayer portrays Jesus's religious power and authority because not only does he depict his authority by accommodating and mimicking Jewish prayers to fit a new situation, but he also, like John the Baptist (Luke 11:1), taught his disciples the Lord's Prayer as a model of how to pray. Hence, by attributing speech to Jesus, the narrative creates the image of Jesus which presents him as a teacher of righteousness. Consequently, this presentation of him contributes to the understanding of the centrality of the figure of Jesus in the early Christian tradition in Mediterranean society.

This application of a narrational inner texture to read the SM presents Matthew's concept of righteousness as an ideology for promulgating his interpretative authority in his community. The teaching of "chreia" in the Matthean Lord's Prayer has a Jewish background, because it shows some commonality with the *Shimoneh Esreh*, for instance. Thus, because Jesus's sayings provide a basis in this model of prayer, ideologically in Matthew's audience the Matthean Lord's Prayer which also sets forth another act of righteousness (6:1), presents a cultural model of prayer provided by Jesus which was relevant to Matthew's audience and complementary to Jewish prayers. Moreover, in terms of the speech of Jesus, not only does Matthew assume the authority to instruct his community to embrace behaviors and attitudes outlined in the Beatitudes (Matt 5:3-12), but he also encourages them to practice and teach Jesus's interpretation of the Torah and participate in acts of righteousness, such as forgiving other people's indebtedness (6:12), and generally acting as members of God's household (6:9; 12:50).

3.2 Conclusion

The application of inter textual analysis for reading Matthew's version of the Lord's Prayer has indicated that progression derived from the repetitive pattern, opening-middle-closing and narrational textures point to the centrality of Matthew's use of his version of the Lord's Prayer to espouse the rhetorical significance of the concept of greater righteousness (Matt 5:20). The Lord's Prayer stands as the author's ideology conveyed by the symbolism of and the speech and actions of both the figure of Jesus and the implied author reflected in the text as a means to expound the significance of greater righteousness (Matt 5:20) contrasted by the public display of the hypocrites and ἐθνικός (gentiles, pagan, unbelievers) way of prayer (6:1–4; 7–8) but symbolized by the prayer done in secret place and in trusting God (6:5–7), in an attitude similar to that of alms giving (6:5–7). The righteousness espoused by the Lord's Prayer entails the author's ideology regarding the identity of the readers not only on account of contrasting the attitude of hypocrites and ἐθνικός with the audience, but also it describes the audiences as members of the God's household (6:9), the reason for which they look unto God for their food and security provisions (6:11–13). This prompts the question: what are the institutions or kind of people that Matthew had in mind that he identifies as τῶν γραμματέων καὶ Φαρισαίων (Teachers of the Law and Pharisees: 5:20), οἱ ὑποκριταὶ (the hypocrites: 6:2) and ἐθνικός (6:7), the reason for which Matthew wanted to use his version of the Lord's Prayer to construct the identity of his community by contesting their acts of righteousness, such as to Prayer and alms giving, with that of the community of Matthew? To this end, we turn to the next chapter to explore the social setting of Matthew's Gospel in order to investigate the socio-economic and political environment that informed identity in the Roman Empire, Diaspora Judaism and the Jesus Movement.

CHAPTER 4

THE SOCIAL SETTING

To explore the social, economic and political strategies that shaped identity of the communities within the vicinity of the community of Matthew in the late first century CE, it is crucial to discuss the social and geographical location of the community of Matthew in Syrian Antioch, strategies for 'assimilation' employed by Rome to effect 'Romanization' in the Roman Empire and, explore the responses of the Judeans in the Diaspora and the Jesus Movement to Roman assimilation on the prospects of their identities.

4.1 Antioch: Geographical and Sociological Composition of Matthew's Community.

Following the evidence within Matthew's Gospel, including Jesus's genealogy, the missionary focus on Jews and Gentiles, and the external evidence from writers such as Ignatius, the provenance of Matthew's Gospel can be identified as Antioch. Josephus suggests that Antioch had a sizable Jewish population that enjoyed some imperial privileges. Similarity between Ignatius's virginal birth report and Matthew's genealogy further explains the significance of Jesus's genealogy (Matt 1:1-11), the missionary focus on Jews (Matt 10:5-6) and ἔθνος (the nations: Matt 28:19-20) as crucial indications of the ethnic identity of the Matthean community in Antioch.

Kuecker tells us that in Antiquity, there were three main categories that described ethnicity. These are ἔθνος which was reserved for non-Greeks, γενος which referred to Greeks, and ὁ λαός which was reserved for Israel. There were also other categories for small tribal groups, such as Pliny's reference to 112 tribes in Northern Italy, 49 gentes in parts of the Alps, 150 populi in Macedonia, and 30 peoples in Crimea.[1] Esler

---

1. Kuecker, "Ethnicity and Social Identity," 62-64.

contends that ἔθνος and γένος can be used as a reference that categorizes these groups in terms of blood and birth. The term Ἕλληνες was used in the Roman Empire to refer to Greeks (from the Roman word Graeci), or people who originated from Graece.[2] Similarly, Ἰουδαῖοι refers to people who originated from Ἰουδαία (Judah) and associated themselves with the temple in Jerusalem, although some of them were scattered around the Mediterranean world.[3] When the concepts such as Ἕλληνες, Ἰουδαῖοι, and ἔθνος and ὁ λαός are used, they are referring to superordinate categories comprised of sub-groups like the Jesus Movement, which was comprised of several sub-groups, referred to as early Christian communities. The letters of Ignatius are important in providing more insight into the character and identity of the early Christian communities found in Antioch in the late first-century CE.

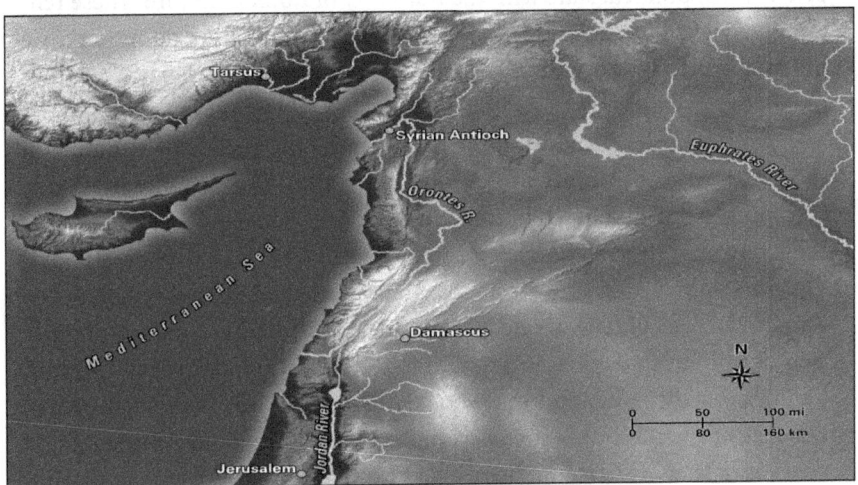

Figure 2. Map of Syrian Antioch[4]

Antioch of Syria is located along the Orontes River in modern-day Turkey. Antioch, which was a Hellenistic city, during time of the New Testament, had become a center of commerce and a crucial political power in the Roman Empire. Although Antioch was separated by hundreds of miles from Jerusalem, a noteworthy Judean population had settled there by the

2. Esler, *Conflict and Identity*, 54–55.
3. Esler, *Conflict and Identity*, 63–65.
4. Fogg, "Antioch."

second century BCE. Herod the Great paved the main streets of Antioch with marble. The city also became a center for early Christianity, playing a prominent role in the ministry of the apostle Paul in the New Testament. According to the book of Acts, it was at Antioch that followers of Jesus were first called Christians (Acts 11:26) and had become Paul's center for mission to the Gentiles (Rom 15:25–29; Gal 2:11–14).[5]

Ignatius's (*Smyr.* 1.1–2) references to the virginal birth of Jesus and the proclamation of universal salvation for both Jews and Gentiles confirms the presence of the Gospel of Matthew, because these bear similarities to Matthew's genealogy of Jesus (Matt 1:18–22). Josephus (*BJ* 7.43) insinuates that by the mid-first century CE the Jewish population in the city of Antioch ranged between twenty-five and sixty thousand people. Religious rights for the Jews in Antioch were granted by the Roman government under the privileges of political state with the fraternity of Roman Empire. These religious privileges included freedom to keep Jewish Sabbath, exemption from military conscription and permission to perform other Jewish religious practices (Josephus, *AJ* 12.119; *BJ* 7.43).

Rodney Stark provides some insights into the social environment of the Matthean community in Antioch. According to Stark, the Matthean community formed part of the multi-ethnic society in Antioch that ranged from retired soldiers, Jews from Palestine, Syrian natives, slaves of diverse origin, Gauls, and Germans, among others. Life in Antioch posed a high risk of epidemics and social tensions, because it had a population density of 205 persons per acre, poor sanitation, poor water supply, a high mortality rate, and an average life span of less than thirty years. Because of the miserable social-economic environment in Antioch, Stark concludes that "Christianity provided a revolutionary response that revitalized a Roman world groaning under a host of miseries."[6] Going by the socially deplorable environment of Antioch in the late first century, not only did early Christianity become a factor in revitalizing life and hope, but because it operated as a superordinate group of the Jesus Movement that was not ethnically bound, it provided a new communal identity and a place of belonging in Antioch. Rodney Stark, in his description of the socially deplorable condition of Antioch, paints a picture of a city experiencing social chaos because of its overcrowded population with

---

5. Fogg, "Antioch."
6. Stark, "Antioch," 191–200.

concomitant health hazards that would have caused despair and danger to a city in desperate need of revitalization.

A revisit to recategorization into a superordinate identity will help us to explain the rhetorical role of Matthew's version of the Lord's Prayer in constructing the identity of the Matthean community in Antioch. A superordinate identity entails embracing a socially reconstructed identity alongside an essentialist identity (such as an ethnic or race-based identity) and thus supersedes all other identities. Because it embraces more than one category, a superordinate identity has the potential to reduce ethnic-based tensions and conflicts.[7] However, this does not mean that superordinate identity should be glorified. When embracing the "in-group" and "out-group", there might be conflict, which can be attributed to the dynamics of embracing the in-group and out-group to become one community.

Therefore, after one has joined a superordinate group, the situation of interacting with other groups, which might produce nostalgic feelings for the previous identity, should not be overlooked. The case of Jews who became Christians but did not want to lose their Judean ethnic identity is a good example of this (Gal 2:15–16). The solution proposed for this problem is the re-categorization of various groups into a superordinate group to include both the in-group and out-group.[8] Given the multi-ethnic composition of Antioch, the following questions are important; how did the Jesus Movement attempt to handle the multi-ethnic composition of its communities? Would the re-categorizing of the community into a superordinate group work well for all sub-ethnic groups, or were there intra-group conflicts within the superordinate category that required further recategorization? What about Matthew? Was he attempting to use his Gospel to recategorize his community at a superordinate level?

McDonald describes the nature of early church ministry in Antioch during the late first century CE. He observes that the church in Antioch accepted Nicholas, "a proselyte of Antioch," to perform the church ministry (Acts 6:7) just as Paul and Barnabas were doing. By so doing, the "church at Antioch [had] initiated the first international . . . mission."[9] McDonald suggests that although the church in Antioch belonged to the Jesus Movement, in its outreach programs it was mindful of its own multi-ethnic

---

7. Baker, *Identity*, 6–7.
8. Esler, *Conflict and Identity*, 29–30; Faulkner, "Jewish Identity," 7–10.
9. McDonald, "Antioch," 35.

composition; Paul was mostly focused on the Gentile mission, while Peter was focused on the Jewish one (Gal 2:7–8).

The variegated ethnic composition and the myriad of social and economic challenges that the people faced, according to Rodney Stark's analysis of the social setting in Antioch, required different ways of approaching Christianity. From the time of Paul, Peter, and later Ignatius, there were three main approaches to Christian missions in Antioch. First, from the point of view of Gal 2:11–14, 15–21 the apostolic mission represented by Paul was relevant because it mostly addressed a Christian community with less Ἰουδαῖοι (Judean) but more τὰ ἔθνη (the Gentiles). According to Paul, while in Antioch Peter was eating with τὰ ἔθνη, and living ἐθνικῶς (like a Gentile/in contrasts to the Jewish; Gal 2:14). Second, Peter's (and to some extent James') missionary approach was pro-Ἰουδαῖος, which looked as if it was proselytization of τὰ ἔθνη, was pertinent because it appealed mostly to Jewish Christians. Thus, before followers of James arrived, Peter withdrew because of the circumcision faction. This likely refers to Jewish Christians who wanted Gentiles to undergo circumcision to be full members of the Jesus Movement. Circumcision of Gentile Christians was important in meeting Rome's requirements of Judean identity for Christians. Winter, following Robbinson, claims that Christians in Galatia were compelled to circumcise Gentile Christians "to escape possible prosecution in the Roman province of Galatia," because "the circumcision party would have to be able to show they qualified as a legitimate Jewish association."[10] The third missionary approach in Antioch was provided by Matthew's Gospel, which focused both on Ἰουδαῖοι' (Matt 10:5–6) and τὰ ἔθνη communities (Matt 4:24; 28:19–20).

Besides a Jewish populace, there were also three predominant forms of Christianity in Antioch in the late first-century: apostolic, gnostic and Jewish Christianity. These three forms of early Christianity most likely provided three corresponding perspectives that informed the formation of Christian identity, which flourished within the city of Antioch. First, Eusebius (*Hist.* 3.3.5; 3.36.2–3) who was active in the late third and fourth century CE suggests that apostolic Christianity started to take root in Antioch after Paul's death. Second, gnostic Christianity, which denied the full divinity of Jesus Christ, remained part of the early Christian community in Antioch even though Paul and Ignatius (*Mag.* 8.1; *Trall.* 10.1; *Smyr.* 2.1—4.1) discouraged its presence. Third was Jewish Christianity (Ignatius, *Mag.* 8.1; 10:2–5; *Phil*

---

10. Winter, *Divine Honours*, 243.

6.1). In *Magnesians* 10, Ignatius was trying to suppress Jewish Christianity by attacking Judaizing motives. Because of these three forms of Christianity, it is not surprising to learn that Paul's letter to the Galatians, the Gospel of Luke, and the Gospel of Matthew, which McDonald believes were composed around 75–90 CE,[11] were all produced in Antioch to address the concerns of the apostolic, gnostic and Jewish communities.

The above observations help illustrate the social setting of the community of Matthew in Antioch. However, although the role of Diaspora Judaism and that of the other early Christian communities (the Jesus Movement) in shaping the content of Matthew's Gospel, has been briefly explored above, very little attention is paid to the role of the Roman Empire in shaping the discourse of the Matthean community, an issue which has been addressed by Warren Carter. Carter argues that vertical exertion of Roman power through the elites was responsible for the horizontal, verbally communicated violence in the Gospel of Matthew. He argues that the existence of a synagogal-Matthew conflict attests not primarily to a religious strife but elite or imperial pressure. Imperial negotiation or elite-non-elite status supplies the primary axis for understanding of the Gospel's context and content of this conflict.[12] Compared to Meier and Overman, Carter provides a better approach, regarding the Gospel of Matthew as a reflection of the socio-economic and political Roman imperial strategy of assimilation to which both Diaspora Judeans and the Jesus Movement were responding. To be noted here is Carter's use of the word "negotiation." According to him, he uses the term "not to mean formal face-to-face discussions between Christian leaders and imperial leaders, but to refer to making one's way or shaping an appropriate way of life and identity in the midst of the Roman Empire."[13]

Guided by this definition of negotiation, Carter summarizes the Gospel of Matthew as reflective of the negotiation of Roman imperial power via four contested dimensions, namely: (1) Matthew's genealogy (Matt 1:1–17) that makes several claims against the Roman empire; (2) God's sovereignty, blessings and will (Matt 1:2; 4:17; 5:3–12) by which Matthew discredits synagogue communities; (3) practices of crucial self-definition, such as Sabbath observance (Matt 12:3–5), which echoes Hosea 6:6, insisting on a transformative claim, and (4) Matthew legitimates leadership that

11. McDonald, "Antioch," 35.
12. Carter, "Matthew," 286.
13. Carter, "Matthew," 287.

interprets the tradition by affirming Jesus's authority as God's faithful agent (Matt 1:18–25; 3:13–17; 4:1–11) while discrediting various Jewish leaders and synagogues (Matt 5:20; 23:1–34). This reveals an extensive, intensive, and competitive internal contest over the power of the tradition.[14] Carter's concept of negotiation, along with four additional categories; mimicry/imitation, contest, accommodation, and acculturation, will be combined with Social-Identity Theory derived from Tajfel and Turner, Hogg and Mullin, and Baker,[15] to elaborate Matthew's polemical approach to the construction of identity in his community. This interpretive approach is also useful for advancing some of Overman's and Meier's as discussed in chapter 5. The overall argument advanced here is that the narrative of the Lord's Prayer depicts the author's perspective on identity politics. Matthew employs the Gospel narrative for ideological purposes which helps negotiate the socio-economic and political issues emerging from the Roman Empire among Diaspora Judeans and members of the Jesus Movement. This negotiation is achieved through mimicry/imitation, contest, accommodation, and/or acculturation. The purpose of this negotiation is to construct a distinct cultural identity for the Matthean community.

The construction of identity in Matthew's Lord's Prayer in relation to post-70 Diaspora Judaism, like the case with the community's relations with the Roman Empire and the Jesus Movement, identity formation concerns how Matthew presents and constructs a 'version of Judaism.' This method

---

14. Carter, "Matthew," 308.

15. Tajfel and Turner observe that belonging to a group is enough to trigger intergroup discrimination favoring the "in-group" (Tajfel and Turner, "Social Identity," 13). This indicates the conviction that identity formation is shaped by intergroup relations. People express self-understanding in contrast to an out-group. Thus, social identity indicates that group relations are significant for enforcing identity formation in the context of an "us-them" binary. Furthermore, proponents of social identity theory propose two reasons for which people seek to achieve positive social identity: (1) people seek positive social identity in order to foster self-esteem and (2) the functions of norms in group belonging helps avoid uncertainty about entrenched behavior. Consequently, adherents of social identity theory propose that the process of identity formation involves a three-fold recategorization process: (1) a process of depersonalization facilitated by group norms, in which case personal identity is subsumed by the characteristics of a group category; (2) identification with a superior group to maintain self-esteem and reduce subjective uncertainty (Tajfel and Turner, "Integrative Theory"; Kuecker, "Ethnicity and Social Identity," 70–71), and (3) a two-fold social memory theory constituted of a communicative memory characterized by face-to-face experiences of an event, and a cultural memory communicated to future generations through text, rituals and images (Baker, *Identity*, 14–15; Baker, "Narrative-Identity Model," 109–12).

is a mixture of polemics, indebtedness, distancing, aligning, borrowing and differentiation. The relationship between Matthew's community and post-70 Diaspora Judaism, the Jesus Movement and the Roman Empire is sometimes negotiated in the context of conflict. For instance, the nasty attacks of 6:2, 5 (cf. Matt 23). There is also the context of interpretation as in 5:17–20, 21–48; and borrowing from Judaism, such as in 5:3–12 and 6:1–18. This borrowing is seen, for instance, from Psalm 37 and from three common practices of Jewish righteousness, namely; almsgiving, prayer and fasting. Matthew's use of ideology to construct his community's identity is not monolithic and relentlessly oppositional, but as with Roman power and structures and the Jesus Movement, there is multivalent negotiation going on in Matthew's ideological strategy of identity construction. With this brief social context in mind, I will turn to the prospects of identity in Rome, Diaspora Judaism and the Jesus Movement to use some literary witnesses in order to further elaborate dynamics of the social setting of Matthew's community in the late first century CE.

4.2 Identity in Rome, Diaspora Judaism, and the Jesus Movement.

For quite some time, Biblical Scholars have been employing Biblical text to infer the relations between early Christian movements and first century Judaism. This inference is used to decipher the relations between the Jesus Movement, which started in the Jewish homeland, early Christianity, and first-century CE Judaism. The focus on inferring relations between the Jesus Movement, first-century Judaism, and the Roman Empire using Biblical text, began to emerge at the beginning of the twentieth century. In his recent article, "The New Testament as Political Documents," Jeremy Punt complains that, the political nature of the NT documents is carefully hidden away in the folds of a centuries-long tradition of Christianizing and spiritualizing the NT."[16] Punt points out the failure of Biblical scholarship to observe the entwining of socio-economic, political, and religious discourses as a source for communal identity in the world of antiquity. This leads to the question: how did the multivalent nature of religious discourse, in terms of its socio-economic and political perspective, influence communal identity formation in the Roman Empire, Diaspora Judaism, and the Jesus Movement in the first century CE? To answer this question, the basis

16. Punt, "New Testament," 1.

of identity formation in the Roman Empire has to be studied before exploring its role in the formation of identity in Judaism and the Jesus Movement in the first century CE. Prior to doing this, a brief overview of current New Testament scholarship regarding the Roman Empire will be helpful in providing the scholarly context for this discussion of identity.

4.2.1 Trends in New Testament Scholarship regarding Roman Empire Theories

Classical work of Suetonius and the recent work of Duling and Esler provide a scholarly view that details some of the current concerns in New Testament studies regarding the development of a hybrid identity in the process of negotiating the Roman Empire as a dominant power during the emergence of the Jesus Movement.

In "Empire: Theories, Methods, Models," Duling follows Karl Wittfogel, S. N. Eisenstaedt, and Gerhard Lenski to define and explain the emergence of the term "empire" in order to illustrate both the vertical and horizontal dimensions of the hierarchy in Roman imperialism in the Gospel of Matthew. Duling's research significantly contributes to the present discussion in two ways: First, his conclusion that the exertion of the Roman hegemonic power in the first century through the Jewish aristocracy provoked three forms of peasant resistance-millennial movements, peasant revolts, and everyday non-violent resistance, summarizes the kind of resultant hybrid identity expressive of the inherent power in the negotiation of the social and cultural values emerging from the Roman Empire.[17] The resultant hybrid identity of the Matthew's community can be classified as a millennial movement that preferred a response of non-violent resistance to Rome. This is indicated by the fact that the SM emphasizes forgiveness and love of one's enemy (Matt 5:43–48; 6:10). This non-violent attitude is grounded in the literary context of suffering for righteousness (Matt 5:10–12) and eschatological relief from suffering (Matt 24:30–31; 25:32–46). Second, Duling claims that in the Roman Empire, "Ethnic self-identity was corroborated by Roman imperial theology."[18] He concludes that the Romans, particularly in the eastern part of the Empire, "believed that they [Romans] were God's chosen people and that if their leaders, especially the emperor, maintained the appropriate virtue and piety their mandate to rule the world was a

---

17. Duling, "Empire," 73–76.
18. Duling, "Empire," 73–76, following Carter, *Matthew and the Margins*, 20–29.

mandate from heaven."[19] Duling suggests that the Romans believed that if they and their emperors remained pious and virtuous, they would continue to be chosen by the gods to rule over the world.

Thus, Duling's suggestion shows that the Roman imperial theology was applied by the Roman Emperors and elites in Rome as a motivation to maintain harmony in the Roman Empire. Duling also implies that Roman imperialism was a symbol of political ideology that attempted to construct, for the first time, a common identity for Roman citizens (this did not include the non-Roman people living in the empire) across a wide range of ethnic groups dispersed over thousands of kilometers.

In his study, Duling attempts to examine to what extent religious freedom granted by the Roman emperors contributed to the shaping of Matthew's Gospel narrative, which introduces Jesus as having a special divine status as *Ima-nu-el* (God with us: 1:23) before he is portrayed as greater than Moses (5:1–2). According to the Gospel of Matthew, Jesus had the authority not only to interpret the Law (5:17–20) but to give instructions concerning almsgiving, prayer, and fasting (6:1–18). This special divine status accorded to Jesus in Matthew's narrative provided a mode of identity formation for the Matthean community. Matthew's negotiation with respect to religious freedom granted by Rome was a means to forge a common hybrid identity for his community. This shows how important it is to consider the Roman Empire as the historical context for early Christian discourse as reflected in the New Testament. The negative impact of the avoidance of references to the Roman Empire as the historical context for early Christian discourse by New Testament scholars has been noted by Richard Horsley:

> The basic assumptions and controlling concepts of the field of New Testament studies obscured the Roman Empire as the historical context of Jesus and the Gospels. New Testament studies developed in Western Europe as the division of theology that interpreted the sacred texts of the Christian religion. Religion was understood as separate from political-economic affairs. Religion was also increasingly understood as individual faith or belief. Correspondingly, New Testament books were defined as religious texts about religion, the Gospels viewed as merely collections of the sayings of and stories about Jesus, and Jesus understood as an individual teacher of individuals.[20]

---

19. Duling, "Empire," 74.
20. Horsley, "Jesus-in-Movement," 47.

The ignoring of the Roman Empire as the historical context for early Christian discourse by some modern scholars has limited our understanding of the world in which Christianity emerged by presenting a monolithic view of religious discourse disinterested in the socio-economic and political experiences of the time.

Some classical writers, such as Suetonius, seem to give the wrong impression of how the Roman Empire featured in the emergence of early Christian discourse, particularly with reference to the Flavian dynasty. Suetonius's (*Dom.* 13.2) misrepresentation of emperor Domitian creates the impression that the Roman Empire, particularly the Flavian dynasty, employed the emperor cult to enforce Rome's dominance in the Empire. Suetonius's misrepresentation of Domitian's reign and personality has been a subject of discussion among New Testament scholars, such as Leonard L. Thompson[21] and Geoff W. Adams.[22]

Suetonius's false impression of the supposed excesses of Domitian and the Flavian dynasty, of which Domitian was the last member, is exacerbated by modern scholars such as Philip Esler and Dennis Duling. Esler suggests that after their conquest of Greece, the Romans continued to sustain their political dominance through unmitigated military violence towards conquered cities and their people; they raped women and killed many or the entire population to sustain their political dominance in the Empire.[23] Similarly, grounding his argument in Doyle and Woolf, Duling asserts that to sustain its dominance, the Roman empire employed an imperial ideology that combined Roman ethnicity and imperial theology to control people, beliefs, religions, laws and monetary systems.[24] Not only did writers from antiquity such as Suetonius and some modern scholars such as Esler and Duling represent Rome as imposing its will on the citizens, but also they collectively promote a monolithic view of Roman religion, which in effect conceals the entwining of socio-economic and political issues with religious experiences in the Roman Empire.

Furthermore, in the Roman Empire religion was entwined with the socio-economic and political functions of the Empire whereby the interconnection between culture, identity, and power facilitated Rome's acceptance of the practice of various religious cults by the local communities,

---

21. Thompson, *Revelation*, 95–115.
22. Adams, "Suetonius," 1–13.
23. Esler, "Rome," 11–12.
24. Duling, "Empire," 73.

even though public religion in the provinces was administered by Roman officials. Thus, the contribution of this section is guided by the question: how did the Roman emperors enforce their agendas in the Empire, and how did this approach impact on peoples' cultural identity? Consequently, I argue that the Roman Empire employed multivalent nature of religion, that is, the socio-economic and political interconnectedness of religion to provide the grounds for the formation of people's cultural identity and religious freedom.

In Antiquity, identity formation happened on account of one's relations to other people, places and things. Malina and Neyrey have observed that in Antiquity narratives of collective identity, rather than an individual's choice, were guided by belonging to a fictive family, a city dwelling, or political factions or coalitions, played a significant role in the formation of an individual's social identity.[25] In Rome, the elite and local communities played a significant role in cultural identity formation in the Empire. I proceed by outlining Janet Huskinson's and Michael Mann's empire theories to provide a lens to help demonstrate the socio-economic and political interconnectedness of religion in the Roman Empire. Then, I will outline the cultural identity formation of first-century Diaspora Judaism and the Jesus Movement.

4.2.2 Identity Formation in the Roman Empire

4.2.2.1 *Janet Huskinson and Michael Mann's Empire Theories*

In her essay, "Looking for Identity, Culture, and Power," Janet Huskinson presents her theory of empire by first defining "culture" as "shared meanings" based on her conviction that when people belong to a particular cultural group they "share a set of assumptions and experiences . . . expressed by following certain common practices or by employing accepted representations of mutual identity."[26] It is this aspect of a "shared set of assumptions and experiences" which can help detect cultural values in the Roman Empire in terms of Rome, the Roman elites, and local communities. Having defined culture in her theory of empire, Huskinson's view of cultural diversity[27] plays a significant role in establishing the commonality

---

25. Malina and Neyrey, *Portraits of Paul*, 154–64.
26. Huskinson, "Looking for Identity," 5.
27. Cultural diversity entails common membership in Roman culture, which is

of Roman culture in the Empire.[28] This commonality is also described as "Romanization," a process by which Roman culture spread across the empire through "assimilation," "imitation" and "acculturation," as explained via essentialist,[29] and relativist[30] perspectives. Although essentialism forms an important part of Huskinson's theory, it is not a modern concept. Essentialism can be inferred from the significance of the concept of "Romanization" because, as already noted by Huskinson, in the Roman world some indigenous groups claimed essential distinctiveness in terms of their past, usually as a survival strategy in the face of the dominant Roman culture. According to Huskinson, such distinctiveness was claimed "by promoting the myths" attached to the foundations of cities, and by presenting local gods or heroes in public ritual and art.[31] In Huskinson's theory, some aspects of "power relations" are present. While the perception of cultural identity is expressed through personification,[32] representation and self-

represented by shared values such as language, religion, names, dress, codes of morality, and ancestral customs. Huskinson, "Looking for Identity," 7.

28. How did "Romanization" as a process, whereby Roman culture was spread across the Empire take place? Huskinson suggests that assimilation is one of the means by which Roman culture spread. Assimilation could happen either through a pattern of imitation or acculturation whereby the non-Roman local elites adopted for themselves some of the Roman practices in order to leverage social status. Thus, "Romanization" involved the military, religious, legal, and administrative civil institutions, and their building projects and ceremonies. Huskinson, "Looking for Identity," 21.

29. According to Huskinson, from an essentialist perspective, aspects such as ethnicity and sex, which from a biological point of view are non-negotiable, provide the basis for a definition of cultural identity. Huskinson, "Looking for Identity," 10.

30. In terms of the relativist view, cultural identity in the Roman Empire was not understood as determined by biological attributes but was treated as a fluid category, determined by social context in which, for example, certain types of behavior or situations constructed identities of male or female. In reference to Roman cultural identity, the concept 'Romanization' borders on essentialism because Roman cultural identity is grounded in the argument that there was a homogenous and identifiable Roman culture. Huskinson, "Looking for Identity," 10–11. Huskinson utilizes the concept of essentialism, which some modern scholars reject, alongside social constructivism and relativism to explain her perspective of cultural identity formation.

31. Huskinson, "Looking for Identity," 12.

32. How did the people in the Roman Empire perceive identity? Huskinson's view is that cultural identity is the perception of other people as with one's own perception. Huskinson says that in the Roman Empire, identity was perceived in terms of the provinces being included in the culture of the empire. This perception is communicated through personification. For instance, this is visible in the mosaic floor tiles in the depiction of Thysdrus, in modern El Djem in Tunisia. Africa is represented as a woman with idealized features such as wearing classical dress. Her ethnic features are

representation, the motives for cultural identity, are ideologically demonstrated in the light of power relations in the Roman Empire.[33] While Huskinson's theory is helpful in providing some insights on how essential cultural attributes, such as one's ethnicity and race, inform social identity, she has not clearly elaborated how minority groups exert their social power in the context of a dominant cultural group.

In addition to Huskinson's theory, Michael Mann provides another theory of empire that supplements Huskinson's view of power by extending it to include military and political aspects in addition to ideological and economic ones. In Mann's view, these four sources of social power, that is; ideological, economic, military and political power, are not independent, they are entwined. That is, their interactions change one another's inner shape as well as their outward trajectory.[34] This in effect shows the multivalent character of social power that can also be applied to explain the nature of cultural identity formation in the Roman Empire. Consequently, Huskinson presents three concepts that are helpful in explaining the construction of cultural identity, namely; culture, identity and power. Mann's four subcategories; ideological, economic, military and political, are useful for elaborating these three major categories of cultural identity formation. This will be done in terms of the interaction between the place of Rome, provincial elites, the local communities, and the imperial cult in the formation of cultural identity in the Empire.

4.2.2.2 *Rome*

The nature of Roman cultural identity is informed not only by the role of the Roman officials, but also through the conspicuous geographical, social, religious, economic and political functions of Rome, her provincial elite, and local communities. This focus on Rome leads to the question: what was the contribution of Rome in the formation of cultural identity in the Empire? Rives answers this question by pointing out the role of elites in Rome saying that

> in Rome ... public religion was organized and maintained by the political and economic elite: they made all the important decisions

---

symbolized by the elephant-skin headdress which emphasizes distinctiveness. Huskinson, "Looking for Identity," 14.

33. Huskinson, "Looking for Identity," 15–17.
34. Mann, *Sources of Social Power*, 1–3.

while the priests and magistrates (who were themselves senators) maintained the traditional religious prescriptions and performed the rituals. In this respect public religion was no different from foreign policy of governance of the city.[35]

Thus, Rome seems to have been a center not only of political issues but also of religious and economic matters. This is most likely the reason that religion in the Roman Empire was embedded within economic, political and civic life.

In classical literature, Virgil, Columella, Josephus, and Tacitus have been selected among others such as the Psalm of Solomon, Livy, Dionysius of Halicarnassus, and Horace, to provide the late-first century CE evidence regarding the role of Rome in shaping cultural identity in the Empire. Some scholars are known to have a certain mistrust of Josephus, because they argue that he was a puppet of the Flavian dynasty since he wrote under the patronage of Vespasian. To allay these fears and boost the credibility of Josephus's evidence, it is crucial to consult other classical writers who write before Josephus, such as Virgil and, those who write around the same time with Josephus, such as Tacitus and Columella.

Josephus embarked on his career of writing the history of the Jews after Vespasian spared his life following his capture by Vespasian's soldiers during the 66–73 Jewish revolt. He settled in Rome to write the history of the Jews. Josephus tells us that, in the pre-70 CE period, Rome was reasonably tolerant of local religions. Jewish priests were allowed to offer sacrifices and encourage the Jewish people to worship in Jerusalem, as long as some accommodation was reached that recognized Roman power by the Jews. This is one case that demonstrates Rome's tolerance of Jewish representation of Jewish cultural identity in the light of the Jerusalem temple and its priesthood in the context of Jewish monotheism and non-image-oriented worship. Although the Jewish chief priest was appointed by Rome, they were nevertheless obliged to guide the Jews in their socio-economic and religious activities. Not only did Rome provide a social environment conducive for worship and socio-economic engagement in Jerusalem, they also provided military security that ensured peaceful celebrations of Jewish festivals, which were often disrupted by seditious groups. By allowing the Jews to worship in Jerusalem according to Jewish traditions, and even providing them with security to counter any disruption, Rome assisted in creating a religious and economic environment whereby the Jerusalem temple, chief priests, and the

---

35. Rives, "Religion in the Roman World," 255.

festivals played a crucial role in facilitating norms, beliefs and traditions that significantly contributed to the maintenance of Judean cultural identity. In this context, Judean cultural identity means an identity of the Judeans that was shaped by a focus on Jerusalem, with its priesthood at the center of people's socio-economic and political beliefs and practices.

Not only did Rome cater for the people's religious activities for the purposes of representing their cultural identity, but as the city of the Empire Rome also facilitated the social aspect of religion. Religion in Rome was a social event that brought people from various ethnic, educational, and economic backgrounds to socialize together irrespective of their difference in religious affiliation. For instance, during the annual celebrations of the *Ludi Romani*, people came from all over the Empire to honor the god Jupiter Optimus Maximus by sacrificing to him and playing games. During the annual celebration of the great Ludi Romani, the annual Roman games celebrated in honor of Jupiter Optimus Maximus, connected Rome to social events facilitated by the interaction of the people originating from different parts of the Empire coming together for the celebration in Rome. While the religious aspect of the Ludi Romani festival was demonstrated by the celebrations that began with an elaborate procession to the Circus Maximus composed of magistrates, performers, and statutes of the gods, and climaxed in a series of sacrifices, the social aspect was composed of the continuation of the festivals for sixteen days after the sacrifices, when chariots races, athletic contests, and theatrical displays would take place.[36]

Not only did these annual celebrations of the *Ludi Romani* festivals have a religious and social aspect, but the festivals incorporated certain ideological power relations. Because the celebration was performed in honor of Jupiter, the superiority of Jupiter and his worshipers over other gods and their local worshipers in the rest of the Empire was demonstrated. Not only did worshipping Jupiter legitimate a Roman cultural identity, it also likely provided a more prestigious basis of cultural identity in the Empire because of its connection to Rome, more than belonging to local communities that only worshipped local deities.

In addition to Josephus's narratives concerning cultural identity in Rome, Virgil is also a reliable source. Although Virgil (c. 70–19 BCE) lived much earlier than either Josephus or Suetonius, his poetry, particularly the *Aeneid*, is a profound source of socio-economic and political narrative of the early Roman Empire. In his *Aeneid* (6.852), Virgil, in his celebration

---

36. Rives, "Religion in the Roman World," 253–54.

of the power relations embedded in Rome's relations with the rest of the Empire and beyond, declared, "you, Roman, be sure to rule the world (be these your arts), to crown peace with justice, to spare the vanquished and to crush the proud." Huskinson attempts to explain the multivalent nature of the power relations between Rome and the rest of the Empire in her analysis of the El Djem Floor Mosaic (below), which depicts the goddess Roma in the center of the tiles, surrounded by six figures of deities which represent the provinces of the Roman Empire.

Figure 3: The El Djem Floor Mosaic

Confirming the asymmetric nature of these power relations, as well as their effect in maintaining a distinctive Roman culture and political power in the Empire, illustrated by the above El Djem Floor Mosaic (fig. 3), Huskinson remarks that the foreigners of the individual provinces were kept separated and thus peripheral to Rome. This was not only to allow Rome to exercise control from the center, but also to curtail any threats of cultural contamination.[37] Thus, although Rome depended on the provinces for its survival, in the context of controlling its own influences in the

---

37. Huskinson, "Looking for Culture," 17–18.

Empire, it clearly occupied a more honorable and powerful place than the depiction of the provinces in the mosaic of El-Djem.

In the Roman Empire, religion was linked with economic activities which provided sources for maintaining cultural identity. Perkins defines economy from *Oikonomia* as "household or estate management" that can extend to a political economy. In this case, if political economy refers to, "the management of the resources and wealth of a people and of its government," given that in the Roman empire, religion encompassed all spheres of life, then some economic practices could point to religious convictions and norms of a particular group of people.[38] Some economic practices found in the Roman Empire point towards certain religious beliefs of a community which are directly related to such economic practices. This idea is confirmed by Virgil (70–19 BCE), in his *Georgics* (1.26–37), a poem set in the countryside:

> [A]nd you, Silvanus, with a young uprooted cypress in your hand; and gods and goddesses all, whose love guards our fields—both you who nurse the young fruits, springing up unsown, and you who on the seedlings send down from heaven plenteous rain! And you above all, Caesar, whom we know not what company of the gods, shall claim ere long; whether you choose to watch over cities and care for our lands, that so the great globe may receive you as the giver of increase and lord of the seasons, wreathing your brows with your mother's myrtle.

In this poem we see the intertwining of Roman religion with the economy. Virgil attributes the sources of Rome's economy to the agricultural products whose benefactor is the Emperor, understood to be the "giver of increase and lord of the seasons." The notion that the love of Roman goddesses and gods "guards [the agricultural] fields" connects the sources of the agricultural economy to the providential care of the Roman gods. Thus, Rome's economy, which is granted by the emperor as the benefactor, and the Roman goddesses and gods as protectors of the means of economy, reveals the political and religious sources of the Roman economy, respectively. By implication, this notion of the political and religious sources of economy constitutes the norms and traditions that are crucial in the formation and maintenance of Roman cultural identity. To be considered a Roman, it meant acknowledging that people's means of economic survival was bound up with Roman goddesses and gods. Thus, in the Roman Empire, not only was agriculture an important source of people's economic existence, but it

---

38. Perkins, "Power," 183–84.

was also a source for their cultural and religious identity. In the late first-century CE, agricultural economy as normative for the construction of cultural identity in the Roman Empire was noted by Lucius Columella (c. 65 CE), a prominent Roman writer on agriculture. Columella's writing was influenced by Virgil. In his *On Agriculture* (1.5–13), Columella, insisting on an agricultural economy as normative to the cultural identity in the Roman Empire, commented:

> For, even as Marcus Varro complained in the days of our grandfathers, all of us who are heads of families have quit the sickle and the plough and have crept within the city-walls; and we ply our hands in the circuses and theatres rather than in the grain fields and vineyards; and we gaze in astonished admiration at the posturings of effeminate males, because they counterfeit by.

In this case, because agriculture was such an important aspect of the cultural identity in the Roman Empire, Columella laments the departure of the landholders from rural fields in search of work in the non-agricultural sectors of urban society, such as theatres and circuses in the cities. Similarly, people came from all over the Empire for the annual *Ludi Romani* celebrations, for which they would often stay for at least two weeks in Rome, which signifies the nature of Roman religion as a source for economic practices in Rome. During their stay in Rome for *Ludi Romani* festivals, visitors as well as Roman officials mutually benefited through exchange of commodities; olives, ivory, spices, citrus fruits, and clothes would form a better part of the trade that would be going on in Rome during *Ludi Romani*. The economic significance of Rome in the Empire is also illustrated in mosaic floor tiles. Again looking at the floor mosaic of El Djem, Huskinson says that with Rome in the center and Africa and Spain at the periphery, the mosaic represents Africa and Spain as economic partners with Rome who "had great economic power in respect of their exports of grain and oil."[39]

Besides an agricultural economy being a source for cultural identity in Rome, the three principal gods housed in Rome—Jupiter, Juno, and Minerva—also provided a source for cultural identity. The names of these gods could be evoked alongside the gods of the local communities in the various provinces of the Empire. So, why worship Jupiter along with the inferior gods of the local communities? Rives responds to this question, saying:

---

39. Huskinson, "Looking for Culture," 17.

> Romans were quite content to accept that things worked differently in cults from how they did in the myth even if that meant that a god would simultaneously be multiplied and singular, local and universal, that the public cults of Rome could serve as focus for Roman identity even when there were other cults of the same gods in other cities.[40]

By allowing Rome's principle gods to be evoked alongside with other local deities, not only was such evocation expressive of allegiance to the religion practiced in Rome, but it also represented the transformation of religious practices and norms of the local communities through the socio-economic and political values and the beliefs (although the Romans did not have doctrines of belief systems save for cults and myths) associated with these three principal gods. In this case, evoking of the local deities along with Rome's principal gods accomplished two things concerning the supremacy of Rome. One, the evoking of the Rome's principal deities accomplished a political ambition whereby Rome's supremacy was eventually demonstrated over the cities that housed the local deities. Two, in the process of evoking of Rome's deities, even in the provinces, Rome's religious supremacy was achieved by expressing the supremacy of Jupiter, Juno, and Minerva over the local deities. However, this demonstration of the supremacy of Rome did not mean to forcefully subdue the local religious practices. On the contrary; some emperors were known to have been quite friendly to their subjects, including slaves. Tacitus (*Annals* 4.6) noted the cordial economic relations that existed between Emperor Tiberius and the common people, saying:

> The city populace indeed suffered much from high prices, but this was no fault of the emperor, who actually endeavoured to counteract barren soils and stormy seas with every resource of wealth and foresight. And he was also careful not to distress the provinces by new burdens, and to see that in bearing the old they were safe from any rapacity or oppression on the part of governors. Corporal punishments and confiscations of property were unknown.

Tacitus shows how the philanthropic concern of Tiberius revealed his attempt to lessen the economic burden of the common people. For example, by compensating their agricultural failures, "with every resource of wealth" at his disposal. Perkins claims that "this good practice by Tiberius is cited by Tacitus to establish his good conduct as an emperor

---

40. Rives, "Religion in the Roman World," 258.

using his imperial power for the economic benefit of citizens," which in effect demonstrates that the economic benefactors of Roman emperors were in many cases their subjects.[41]

The place of Rome in procuring the socio-economic and political nature of the Empire was briefly discussed above. This socio-economic and political nature provided economic, social, and political norms and values of the Romans which in effect provided grounds for the formation of social identity of individuals and communities in relation to Rome. In this case, the multivalent function of Rome is demonstrated by the annual celebration of *Ludi Romani*, which formed a significant part of the emperor's connection to Rome's principal deities, and his beneficence in terms of meeting the needs of city dwellers and securing the agricultural economy. These are just some of the socio-economic and political values by which Rome provided the basis for people's identity; Rome was not merely a place for expressing these values through ritual but was also a center of authority for approving these values. In this strategy of a multivalent aspect of identity formation in the Roman Empire, the provincial elites also played a significant mediatorial role between Rome and the local communities in the provinces.

4.2.2.3 *The Roman Elites*

Huskinson defines elite culture as "common ground . . . in artistic and intellectual tastes of the elite."[42] Thus, elite culture refers to an almost uniform approach in effecting a mediatorial role between Rome and the local communities in the Roman provinces. The concept of "elite culture" is thus the perception that Roman elites, whether in the western or eastern parts of the Empire, were conduits for a common culture by which they collectively contributed to the process of Romanization. Huskinson's observation regarding Pliny's (*Natural History*) description of Rome's role in unifying and civilizing mankind points to the significance of the common culture of the elite in the Roman Empire in cementing cohesion and cooperation of the privileged classes.[43] Because of its unifying effect, elite culture can be said to have had the ability to construct and maintain a local elite cultural identity in the Empire. Elites participated in Romanization of the Empire

---

41. Perkins, "Power," 196.
42. Huskinson, "Élite Culture," 95.
43. Huskinson, "Élite Culture," 107.

THE SOCIAL SETTING

in several ways that had socio-economic and political dimensions, as exemplified by Virgil, Cicero, Columella and Agricola.

First, Rome attempted to accomplish its socio-economic and political religious interest in the Empire through a special group of Roman elites who operated in the Roman colonies. Rives describes these elites as self-governing communities of Roman citizens that emigrated from Italy to other parts of the Empire.[44] These communities were supposed to be copies of Rome. They were governed by a town council, an equivalent to the Roman senate. These town councils were formed from the political elite with special religious authority. Thus, they were responsible for selecting and overseeing public cults. In these Roman colonies, public cults, like in the case of Roman enfranchised cities, were both Roman and local and so suited to a civic identity that was simultaneously Roman and local.[45] So, by reduplicating Rome's culture, the Roman colonies employed the structures of town councils and public cults to maintain, at the provincial and local levels, a culture similar to the one found in Rome. By implication, these special elites in the Roman Empire would have found it much easier than any other groups annexed by the Empire from outside Rome to reduplicate Rome's socio-economic and political religious values because they were closely connected to Rome. Thus, to sustain their cultural identity that would influence Romanization, the first-generation elites in the Roman colonies did not need to assimilate to any Roman culture, but simply needed to continue practicing religious culture (cult, language and other customs), albeit in new social environment.

Second, Perkins citing Virgil, Cicero and Columella, analyses a villa excavated near Cosa, a Roman Colony, to provide insights for the socio-economic cultural characteristics of Roman elite households. This villa contained two large rooms at its main entrance which housed agricultural machines; an olive mill, an oil press, and three wine presses. The villa is said to have contained all together fifty-two slaves, kept in the villa to provide labour for the household. In view of the slaves and agricultural machines, the villa is indicative of participation in an agricultural economy among members of the Roman elites. Not only were the elite mediators of Rome's political ideology, but they were also conduits of Rome's economic and ideological interests, values and conceptions.[46]

44. Rives, "Religion in the Roman World," 260.
45. Rives, "Religion in the Roman World," 260.
46. Perkins, "Power," 190–93.

Third, besides passing on Rome's economic and ideological interests in the Roman colonies, elite culture was propagated through education and civilization inherited from Greece, particularly among the elites who were not Italians, but other ethnic groups in the western part of the empire. This process of spreading elite culture through assimilation is confirmed by Tacitus when he narrates how his father-in-law, Gnaeus Julius Agricola, performed a Roman imperial assignment in Britain. In this regard, Tacitus (*Agricola* 21) noted that while in Britain, Agricola, a member of the Roman elite

> He likewise provided a liberal education for the sons of the chiefs [of Britain], and showed such a preference for the natural powers of the Britons over the industry of the Gauls that they who lately disdained the tongue of Rome now coveted its eloquence. Hence, too, a liking sprang up for our style of dress, and the 'toga' became fashionable. Step by step they were led to things which dispose to vice, the lounge, the bath, the elegant banquet. All this in their ignorance, they called civilization, when it was but a part of their servitude.

Thus, Tacitus notes that Agricola's conduct as a member of the Roman elite encouraged the Briton elites to assimilate to Roman culture. Agricola imparted social, economic, and cultural values through liberal education for the sons of those chiefs he conquered, embracing Rome's culture, including elegant banquets and adopting the toga. Thus, Huskinson aptly observed that the example of Agricola by Tacitus "introduces themes of culture and status . . . within a Roman elite identity, and how elite culture (of varying kinds) operated within the empire."[47]

Fourth, elite culture was in certain places a blending of various cultures comprised of Greek inherited traditions, Roman traditions and local cultures. Huskinson has noted that individual communities could be mixed in their cultural makeup particularly in large cities, where a mixture of traditions gave individual communities a distinctive culture of their own.[48] This would have likely been the case in Asia Minor and the Near East. Thus, in places like Syrian Antioch, which was part of the eastern empire, an elite culture which was a mixture of Hellenistic and Roman culture could be found.[49] The spread of Roman culture through assimilation was used to promote Roman hegemonic power in the Empire.

---

47. Huskinson, "Élite Culture," 97.
48. Huskinson, "Élite Culture," 108.
49. Huskinson, "Élite Culture," 108; Rives, "Religion in the Roman World," 253.

The above example by Tacitus about Agricola coupled with Huskinson's observations regarding the multi-layered elite culture indicates that no force seems to have been used, to impose Roman cultural identity save for people's desire to embrace the new dominant culture in the context of their own inherited traditions.

Fifth, besides mixed communities, Roman public places provided one of the best opportunities for construction of elite culture as an instrument of expanding Romanization. For instance, Huskinson notes:

> Certainly in provincial cities it must have been hard for anyone to move far from the elite qualities encapsulated in the imperial image. The dominance of this was unavoidable. The official images of the emperors and members of their family were circulated in an organized fashion throughout the empire. The portrait statutes were erected in public places, including theatres and amphitheaters, and smaller images were presented as significant gifts. This was not only by official instigation; local elites also promoted the practice by setting up imperial images alongside their own.[50]

Huskinson suggests that Roman socio-economic elites propagated Roman culture, which led to the so-called Romanization. This process was in part instigated by the presence of imperial iconography in sculpture and coinage that, as a basis of social identity, caused people to identify with the emperor as the face of Roman culture and rule. In this, a connection between social power and the political interest found in elite culture is evident. By this kind of identification with the Roman emperor, not only did the elite manage to elevate their social status, but they were also able to demonstrate their political position and identity in the Empire as mediators of the emperor's political interests, a crucial feature of sustaining elite cultural identity.

Moreover, given this brief exploration of elite culture, without being superficial about late first century CE Romanization, we can confidently conclude that in one way the spread of Roman culture through assimilation has been used to promote Roman hegemonic power in the empire. However, the above example from Tacitus about Agricola coupled with Huskinson's observation regarding the multi-layered elite culture, indicates that no force seems to have been used to expand elite culture; save for people's desire to embrace the new dominant culture in the context of their own inherited traditions. It was important for the elites to stand as conduits for Rome's political, economic and cultural interests, while at the

---

50. Huskinson, "Élite Culture," 109.

same time exuding social power over local communities in the provinces, especially on behalf of the political, religious and economic interests of the emperors and their families. In their social settings, then, Roman elites throughout the empire were better placed to influence the masses than the Emperors, and they could choose to filter down imperial decrees or engage in propaganda to promote certain political ideologies. In this way, a significant feature of elite cultural identity in the Roman Empire was found and sustained through the elites in local communities.

4.2.2.4 Local Communities

The way in which socio-economic elites mediated Roman culture between emperors and local communities, while in the process creating a culture peculiar to an elite identity that granted them a special social status in the Roman Empire has been noted. In what follows, I will briefly explain how local communities received Roman culture to inform and maintain their own cultural identity. Not only did Rome employ assimilation to construct and sustain a cultural identity for and through the elite, but assimilation was also applied to transmit Roman culture to local communities.

Tertullian (160–220 CE), a Christian writer from Carthage in North Africa who lived in the late second and early third century, offers us a depiction of peoples' freedom of worship in the Roman Empire in the late second century and the early third century CE. He observed:

> Every province and city have its proper gods, as Syria the god Ashtaroth, Arabia has Disares, Bavaria Belinus, Africa the Celestial Virgin, and Mauritania their kings. Now these provinces (if I mistake not) are under the Roman jurisdiction, and yet I do not find any of the Roman gods in worship among them. (*Apology* 24.3–4)

Tertullian indicates that Rome did not impose its deities on the various Roman provinces. Despite Rome not imposing its deities in the provinces, Rome did implement *interpretatio*, the practice of identifying a provincial or local deity with Roman deities by superimposing a Roman name over the local one. To illustrate this process of Romanization, Rives cites a case from two Roman provinces, Gaul and Africa. In Gaul, Rives says that *interpretatio* was commonly practiced. For instance, there were dedications of Mars Albiorix, Mars Belado, Mars Camulus, and Mars Giarinus. Rives further says that the effect of this kind of *interpretatio* involved a process of rendering an alien deity by equating it with Roman one. Consequently, this process of superimposing Roman belief systems over local ones, as Rives confirms, resulted to "the native tradition" being "essentially buried underneath the Roman one."[51] This aspect of *interpretatio* was intended to eventually promote Roman religion in local cultures by displacing the local deities with Roman gods. Thus, *interpretatio* stands as another official Roman tool for effecting Romanization through a kind of assimilation that eventually intended to substitute Roman deities and their attendant socio-economic and political nuances for the local ones and their features. By attempting to substitute Roman deities for local ones, the process of *interpretatio* provided a pro-Roman set of norms for grounding the cultural identity of the local communities, albeit in their own local setting. However, *interpretatio* did not always succeed in causing total assimilation to Roman culture, that is, by displacing local deities with a Roman god, as Rive's second case study from the Roman province of Africa shows. Citing a case from Virgil's *Aeneid*, Rives argues that although in Roman poetry the great goddess of Carthage was portrayed as Juno, this was largely ignored in actual cults of Roman Africa, and instead worshipers preferred to use the descriptive name "Caelistis" on its own.[52]

Compared to the case in Gaul, the case of the Caelistis demonstrates that *interpretatio* as a Roman policy of assimilation did not always achieve its intended goal of displacing the deities of local communities with Roman gods. Rather, some communities resisted such assimilation and preferred to pursue their local deities, effectively preserving their local cultural norms as the basis for their identity even as Romanization was taking place around them. Although Rome's authority seems to have been challenged by such resistance, we do not see Rome enacting subsequent policies that forcefully imposed Roman culture on such dissenting groups. This shows that the policy of *interpretatio* was not forcefully imposed on local communities around the empire. The local communities had the freedom to accept or reject the practice of *interpretatio* as a political and religious tool for assimilating local communities into Roman culture. "Roman culture" here refers to a group's predominantly practiced behavior and norms encouraged by Rome as the socio-economic and political center of the Empire. This resistance of Roman official decrees on

---

51. Rives, "Religion in the Roman World," 257.
52. Rives, "Religion in the Roman World," 257–58.

Romanization was most likely to be true in the eastern part of the Empire as confirmed by Rives, who says that in the eastern empire

> Greek myth was adopted and expressed in literature.... Romans even adopted some Greek rituals... to be performed *ritu Graeco*, according to Greek rite.... [P]ublic cults in the Greek world as in Rome were an aspect of civic life, closely associated with particular cities and serving to define and reinforce civic identity.[53]

In this case Rives indicates that Romanization as an official tool for assimilating local communities to Roman culture did not always succeed in displacing local cultures. On the contrary; in cases like the example of Greek culture and Caelistis in Africa, Rome's culture eventually seemed not only to have been resisted but was even influenced by local cultures.

While the above exploration of Rome, Roman elites, and local communities has generally shows how socio-economic and political experiences provided people's basis for cultural identity and social power, it is important to also look at a specific imperial dynasty. A brief look at the Flavian Dynasty will help us to see how in the late first-century, Rome, the socio-economic elites, and local communities provided sources of identity formation in the Empire, at a time when most of the New Testament books, including the Gospel of Matthew, were being composed.

4.2.2.5. *The Flavian Dynasty*

Nilsson, following Hartland, claims that the Roman imperial cult, "lacked all genuine religious content... [and the cult's] meaning lay far more in state and social realms, where it served both to express loyalty to the rule of Rome and emperor and satisfy the ambitions of leading families."[54] Nilsson reiterates the centrality that Rome had in matters of identity in the Empire. The expression of loyalty to the Emperor and his family was an essential mark not only of being a Roman citizen or subject, but also of belonging to local communities acceptable to Rome. In other words; being a loyal member of a local community was tantamount to expressing and maintaining loyalty to the Emperor and his family. This expression of loyalty as a mark of identity in the Roman Empire was emphasized in the Flavian dynasty during the late first century CE. Flavian *lex Irnitana*, or

---

53. Rives, "Religion in the Roman World," 251.
54. Hartland, *Associations*, 119; Nilsson, *Geschichte der griechischen Religion*, 385.

Roman Municipal Law, stipulates the oath for swearing into office of the town magistrate. This confirms Nilsson's claim regarding Roman Law as a basis for identity, particularly an elite cultural identity, during the Flavian dynasty. When taking the oath of office in the Flavian dynasty, *lex Irnitana* 26, cited by Cliff Ando, stipulated that every town magistrate must offer his vow saying in an assembly, "by Jupiter, the divine Augustus, the divine Claudius, the divine Vespasian Augustus, the divine Titus Augustus, the genius of Imperator Caesar Domitian Augustus."[55] While swearing in the name of Jupiter reveals the religious aspect of the ceremony, the connection to the chain of emperors from Augustus to Domitian shows the identification of the magistrate with a political and cultural tradition that legitimated the elite cultural identity of the one being sworn in.

Here there is a close connection between social power and cultural aspects of identity. By virtue of being identified with this Roman tradition of oath-taking, not only does the swearing in reconstruct the elite social status, but also the connection to this entrusts some social power to the elite by granting him the power to arbitrate socio-economic and political issues of the local communities on behalf of Rome. This provokes the crucial question: what did Gaius Suetonius (c. 71–135 CE) mean when he claimed that Domitian, the last and youngest son in the Flavian dynasty, demanded to be addressed across the Roman Empire as "Our Master and our God" (*Dom.* 13.2)?

Suetonius's declaration suggests that not only did Domitian demand divine status, but he created the impression that the Flavian dynasty had imposed emperor worship in the late first- century CE Roman Empire. To answer the question posed here about Suetonius, two issues have to be considered; observations of other Roman writers whose literary works relate to the representation of Roman deities and whether the status of the Roman emperors was regarded as equal to that of Roman gods. One such author is the Roman poet Virgil (70–19 BCE). Virgil noted in his *Aeneid* (1.254), in conferring political authority on Romulus and the Empire, Jupiter declared to Romulus, "For these I set no bounds in space or time; but have given empire without end . . . lords of the world, and the nation." In this case Virgil's myth confirms that not only did Jupiter, on account of his divine virtue, grant political power to the Roman empire, but he also sanctioned the Roman emperors to become masters of the world (but not gods). In other words, Virgil's myth depicts Jupiter holding the highest supreme authority

---

55. Ando, *A Matter of the Gods*, 95.

in the Empire. As a result, Jupiter grants to the emperors pious, socio-economic, and political powers to be masters of the world. Virgil writes his poetry almost eighty-nine years before Suetonius was born. Although his poetry gives the general picture of the Empire, he does not address the Flavian dynasty.

Evidence provided by Roman authors during Domitian's reign, such as Quintilian (c. 35–100 CE) and Publius Statius (c. 45–96 CE), is comparable in their representation of Domitian with those writing after Domitian's reign, like Suetonius, Pliny the Younger (c. 61–113 CE), and Dio Cassius (c. 150–235 CE). By examining these sources, it is possible to understand the motivation behind Suetonius's representation of Domitian. Two issues emerge from this kind of reading.

First, the authors writing during the reign of Domitian seem to praise Domitian for his achievements. Thus, in his *Institutio Oratoria*, praising Domitian for his governance exploits, Quintilian says:

> I have restricted my list of poets to these names, because Germanicus Augustus has been distracted from the study of poetry on which he had embarked by his care for the governance of the world, and the gods have thought it scarce worthy of his powers that he should be the greatest of poets. (*Inst. Orat.* 10.1.91)

In this case Domitian, referred to as "Germanicus Augustus", is praised by Quintilian for his governance skills derived from the study of poetry. These, according to Quintilian, granted Domitian social recognition to be considered "the greatest of poets" which represents Domitian as an example to be emulated by the Roman society. Second, Thompson noted that while celebrating the Domitian's seventeenth consulship in 95 CE, Publius Statius simply referred to Domitian as *vates* (poet) and *dux* (military chief), but never as either *dominus* (Lord/Master) or *deus* (God).[56]

These two examples clearly show that Statius and Quintilian collectively characterized Domitian as a modest statesman, ready to deliver on his role as a benefactor to his subjects. However, Tacitus, Suetonius, and Dio Cassius, who wrote in the post-Domitian period, represent Domitian in negative terms that seem to contradict Statius and Quintilian. Tacitus (*Hist.* 4.51) presents Domitian as the unfavored son of Vespasian in comparison to Titus, to whom his father entrusted the leadership of his army.

---

56. Thompson, *Revelation*, 105.

Suetonius describes Domitian as a violent man (*Dom.* 14.1), in similar terms as Dio Cassius who vilified Domitian as

> not only bold and quick to anger but also treacherous and secretive; and so, deriving from these two characteristics impulsiveness on the one hand and craftiness on the other, he would often attack people with the sudden violence of a thunderbolt and again would often injure them as the result of careful deliberation. (*Rom. Hist.* 67.2.1)

Thus, Dio Cassius and Tacitus, like Suetonius who wrote in the post-Flavian era, paint an extremely negative picture of Domitian. What is the significance of this contrast in the representation of Domitian, the last of the Flavian dynasty, of those Roman authors writing in the time of Domitian with those writing in the post-Domitian period, that is, in Nerva's (96–98 CE) and Trajan's era (98–117 CE)? Thompson says that this contrast serves Trajan's ideological purpose because "the retrospective representation of Domitian and his reign serves as a foil in the present praise of Trajan." That is, "the opposing of Trajan and Domitian in a binary set serves overtly in Trajan's ideology of a new age as well as covertly in his praise."[57] Furthermore, not only did Suetonius negatively represent Domitian alone in his literary works, but recent New Testament scholarship indicates that he also negatively represented other pre-Domitian emperors such as Tiberius, Gaius, Claudius, Nero, and Vitellius.[58] What would have influenced Suetonius to negatively represent particularly Domitian in such unrelenting hatred? Adams attributes this negative representation of Domitian by Suetonius to "senatorial influence" and Suetonius's own damnatio memoriae evident in the literature of the period," and "Senatorial hatred of Domitian" occasioned by Domitian's "preference for pursuing his own ideals and standards and ignoring the suggestions of the senate."[59]

Consequently, these classical sources indicate that Suetonius vilifies Domitian in order to praise Nerva and/or Trajan as well as the senate. This is not only to preserve his job, and in a sense secure some political favors from the post-Domitian emperors, but also to satisfy Trajan's desire for a new order marked by anti-Domitian propaganda. Ironically, this propaganda was applied to promote Trajan's fame at the expense of Domitian character. This begs the question of the existence of an emperor cult during the Roman Empire for which we turn to the observations of Chua and Hartland.

57. Thompson, *Revelation*, 115.
58. Adams, "Suetonius," 1; Jones, *Suetonius*, xv; Townsend, "Suetonius," 91.
59. Adams, "Suetonius," 1–2.

4.2.2.6 Emperor Cult

New Testament scholars proposing imperialism as the historical context for the emergence of Christianity attribute the survival of the Roman Empire to religious pluralism and tolerance. Amy Chua contends:

> For all their enormous differences, every single world hyper power in history . . . was, at least by the standards of its time, extraordinarily pluralistic and tolerant during its rise to pre-eminence. . . . [J]ust as strikingly, the decline of empire has repeatedly coincided with its intolerance, xenophobia, and calls for racial, religious or ethnic purity.[60]

Chua suggests that Rome belongs among the hyper powers that received global recognition for participating in sanctioning religious pluralism and tolerance. Complementing Chua's claim, Hartland outlines three levels by which the Roman imperial cult operationalized cultic associations.[61] These levels in effect affirm Rome's preference and support of religious pluralism and tolerance. The first level is that of provincial cultic associations which were devoted to honoring the emperor in temples built by provincial councils. For example, those built in Asia Minor devoted to the goddess Roma and to Roman emperors, and Roma's temple in Ephesus with the statue of Domitian. The second level is that of civic imperial cults whose goal was to attribute honor to the *Sebastoi* (members of the imperial family) through temples such as the ones devoted to Olympian Sebastoi gods in several locations, including Ephesus and Laodecia. Local shrines and monuments constitute the third level of the emperor cult which was devoted to unofficial honoring of the emperor by small groups, families and individuals. These three levels of cultic associations describe the good will of the Roman Empire in employing the emperor cult to attend to sanctioned religious pluralism and tolerance at various levels of social stratification in the Roman Empire. What is lacking in Hartland and Chua's conceptions of the emperor cult is the socio-economic and political multivalent nature of the cult. These are nuanced by the three social levels of honoring the emperors and their families highlighted by Hartland and Chua.

Honoring of the emperors and members of their families provided certain social norms and traditions that correspondingly constructed three types of cultural identities in the Roman Empire: provincial cultural

---

60. Chua, *Day of Empire*, xxi.
61. Hartland, *Associations*, 122–23.

identity, civic cultural identity and local cultural identity. Underlying these three cultural identities is the theme of hierarchical power relations. At the provincial level, citizens' close association with the Roman principle deities and the emperors themselves provided the impetus for the members of the cult to achieve the highest social status. Members at the civic level, due to their freedom to honor the families of the emperors, ranked second. Finally, the local community, although they had their own freedom to explore private religion, they ranked lowest in terms of social power because they were distant from both the emperors and their families. Participation in the emperor cult, whether at the provincial, civic or local levels, enhanced the social status of these communities by their association with the emperor and his family. The emperor cult in the Roman Empire was not merely a religious phenomenon, but it was also an economic, political and cultural tool for promoting imperial ideology that enhanced people's cultural identity and social positioning in Roman society.

This brief survey of identity formation in the Roman Empire has attempted to describe the role of Rome, elites and local communities in representing, constructing and maintaining a cultural identity in the context of privileged power and the emperor cult. The focus on the Flavian dynasty has helped to show how classical authors like Suetonius could use their elitist position to employ propaganda to defend their cultural identity and the imperial privileges attached to such identity. This survey of representing, constructing and maintaining of cultural identity in the context of imperial propaganda by the elite and their acolytes prompts this question: How did first-century CE Judaism, the emerging Jesus Movement, and the Matthean community respond to the Roman Empire? To answer this question, hybrid identity negotiation during the emergence of first-century Judaism in the Diaspora will be explored before examining identity construction and maintenance in the Jesus Movement.

4.2.3 Negotiating Judean Hybrid Identity in the Diaspora.

In this section, I will explore the development of Jewish identity during the Jewish Revolt against Rome in the period 66–73 CE in order to prepare the grounds for describing the role of Roman assimilation and Jewish cultural traditions in negotiation a Jewish hybrid identity in the Diaspora.

4.2.3.1 *Jewish Identity in the 66–70 CE Period*

The exploration of the development of a hybrid Jewish cultural identity in the Diaspora is introduced by Andrew Overman's *Matthew's Gospel and Formative Judaism*, and in Jacob Neusner's article, "The Formation of Rabbinic Judaism: Yavneh (Jamnia) from A.D. 70 to 100." These scholars provide a brief look at the preferential and unfavorable treatment of the Jews in the Diaspora in the first-century CE. In this section, not only shall I be drawing insights from Overman, but I will also be responding to some aspects of his research by pointing out some of the issues that are significant for the development of a hybrid Jewish cultural identity in the Diaspora that have escaped Overman's attention. Viewed from the context of the aftermath of the destruction of the second temple during the first Jewish war with Rome, cultural identities and polytheism in the Roman Empire posed a challenge to Jewish monotheism. Diaspora Judaism responded by negotiating a Jewish identity through a process of recategorization. Focusing on formative Judaism, as Overman, Riches, and Neusner discuss how the development of post-70 CE Jewish identity risks engaging a phenomenon of Judean community that could only be realistic in the late second and early third century. That is, when Rabbinic traditions had paved the way for determining normativity in post-70 Judaism. Also, the main sources appealed to, for instance by Overman, to defend the case for formative Judaism, are mostly from the second and early third century CE. Thus, this discussion will focus on post-70 Diaspora Judaism instead of formative Judaism in order to analyze negotiation of a Judean identity in the Diaspora during the period in which the Matthean community emerged. "Post-70 Diaspora Judaism" is preferable to "Formative Judaism" because the term "Diaspora Judaism" encompasses a variety of Pre-and Post-70 Jewish sectarian groups operating outside Jerusalem, and "post-70 Diaspora" Judaism is a category that would include second century formative Judaism.

By referring to post-70 Judaism as "formative Judaism," Neusner, Overman and Riches seem to underestimate the multivalent nature of post-70 CE Judaism and the role that assimilation with Roman culture played in development of a hybrid Jewish identity in the post-70 CE period. It is noteworthy at this juncture to consider the preferential and unfavourable treatment of the Judeans in the Diaspora in the first century, and to broaden the spectrum on some of the challenges that the Judeans faced during this period.

THE SOCIAL SETTING

Prior to the 66–73 CE Jewish revolt, Rome had not always been hostile to Judeans. The preferential treatment in the earlier days before the turn of first-century CE was remarkable for Rome's philanthropic treatment of the Judeans. For instance, the Judeans were exempted by the Roman imperial edict from military conscription. They also continued to possess the right of assembly for religious purposes granted in the time of Hyrcanus III, which continued in the time of Augustus (Josephus, *AJ* 14.213–25). Furthermore, Josephus (*BJ* 16.16) testifies to Rome's special treatment of the Judeans. During and after the first Jewish war with Rome in 66–73 CE, this favor seems to have been withdrawn, particularly as demonstrated in the period of Flavian dynasty. Margaret Williams tells us that the first brutal treatment of the Judeans happened in 19 CE, when Tiberius, the adopted son of Augustus, expelled about twenty-five thousand Judeans from Rome, while four thousand male Judeans were conscripted. Those who refused to leave Rome or join the military suffered summary execution.[62] According to Suetonius, another punishment against the Judeans in the Diaspora happened in 41 CE, when Emperor Claudius revoked their right of assembly for religious purposes. Claudius later expelled the Judeans from Rome for their involvement in constant riots in the city (Suetonius, *Claud.* 25.4; Acts 18:1–2). Following the 66–73 CE Jewish revolt against Rome, the Flavian dynasty, particularly Vespasian and Titus, employed measures that were meant to demonstrate total subjugation of the Jews in the Diaspora.

Williams noted that to destroy the major basis for Judeans cultural identity in Diaspora, after the fall of Jerusalem, Vespasian destroyed the Leontopolis temple in Egypt. He also imposed upon all Judeans over three years of age an annual tax payable to Rome to support the services of Jupiter Capitalinus.[63] Although Josephus (*BJ* 7.421–36; *AJ* 13.62–73) discusses construction activities of the Leontopolis temple, Metron Piotrkowski, discounting Josephus's account, argues that "Josephus used an Oniad founding-legend for both his narratives on Onias and his temple, but skewed this source polemically, in accordance with the respective main themes of the Judaean War and the Antiquities."[64] Contrary to Piotrkowski, Williams observed that Titus, like his father Vespasian, implemented two kinds of actions against the Jews. One, to remind the Judeans of their defeat in a more spectacular way, Titus erected in all major cities

---

62. Williams, "Jews and Jewish Communities," 328.
63. Williams, "Jews and Jewish Communities," 329.
64. Piotrkowski, "Josephus," 4.

of the Empire monuments commemorating the defeat of the Judeans by the Flavian dynasty. He also erected the arch of Titus at the main forum in Rome, bearing a depiction of the triumphant Roman soldiers holding the looted temple treasures. In this arch, a seven-branched candle stand, trumpets and a table lain with shewbread are depicted.[65]

Figure 4: The Arch of Titus[66]

In this site, it is noted that the arch was built by Domitian in 82 CE to honor his older brother, Titus, after his death. The arch is important from a historical as well as a religious and political point of view because it represents the glory of the Roman Empire, with Titus being viewed in a god-like way, worshiped for his successes, on one hand. On the other hand, it marks the celebration of a how Titus and his father, Vespasian, conquered the people of Jerusalem who were revolting against their Roman rulers in 66–73 CE.[67]

The arch of Titus and the temple instruments inscribed in it, symbolize not only the defeat of the Judeans, but also the subjugation of the temple of Jerusalem, which was a cradle of Judean cultural identity with its attendant religious, economic, and political implications. Ideologically, the arch of Titus is meant to symbolize asymmetric power relations in which Rome's supremacy against Jerusalem and the whole of the Jewish nation is symbolized

---

65. Williams, "Jews and Jewish Communities," 330–31.
66. Povoledo, "Roman Forum."
67. "Arch of Titus, Rome."

by the positional erection of the temple vessels at the main entrance gate to Rome. Further denigration of the social power of Jerusalem was demonstrated by the mounting of the golden cherubim from Jerusalem at the city gate of Antioch on the Orontes in Syrian Antioch.[68]

Viewed in the context of the above humiliation meted out to the Judeans by the Roman Empire in the late first-century CE, and in the absence of the Jerusalem temple, how did the Jews in the Diaspora negotiate Roman policies of assimilation? Tentatively proposed here is the argument that in the absence of the temple, its rituals, and priesthood, some Judeans succumbed to Rome's strategy of assimilation and integrated with Greco-Roman culture. However, symbolic focus on monotheism enabled many Jews in the Diaspora to preserve a Judean cultural identity. To this end, SRAT will be revisited to orientate the lens that will be used to explore the facilitation of Jewish hybrid identity through cultural assimilation and the maintenance of some Judean cultural practices in the Diaspora.

4.2.3.2 *Cultural Assimilation through Romanization*

Rome, the elites, and local communities played a significant role in the Roman imperial strategy of effecting assimilation into Greco-Roman culture. It is not surprising that many Judeans in the Diaspora had succumbed to this assimilation program. The political, religious and economic aspects of assimilation meant that its impact was felt in all spheres of life. In this case, the first maxim of SRAT, which dictates that *a group's identity construction takes shape through recategorization and depersonalization in order to transcend limitations caused by negative aspects such as racism, ethnicity, and geographical limitations,* is instructive. Assimilation to Roman culture was affected among Judeans in the Diaspora through language, military conscription, education, elite culture, slavery, and employment, among other socio-economic and political aspects. The concept of *assimilation* here refers to the process of "social integration (becoming 'similar' to one's neighbors): it concerns social contact, social interactions, and social practices."[69] That means, because assimilation allowed people to willingly acquire Roman culture, it served a double purpose of attempting to maintain Rome's culture and at the same time maintain a common identity in

---

68. Williams, "Jews and Jewish Communities," 330.
69. Barclay, *Jews in the Mediterranean Diaspora*, 92.

the empire. Thus, assimilation was a Roman imperial socio-economic and political strategy for integrating people into Roman culture.

Williams notes that Greek and Latin language effected the assimilation of the Jews to Roman culture. However, Greek language enjoyed more currency than Latin, not only because it was the language of everyday speech in the east, but also because proceedings in synagogues in the Diaspora were conducted in Greek. This had been the case of Diaspora Jews in the early Hellenistic period so much so that Hebrew, the original language of Judeans, no longer was sufficiently intelligible to many Diaspora Jews. In late third century BCE, the Judeans in Egypt translated the Hebrew Bible into Greek, creating the Septuagint. Furthermore, Jewish use of the Greek language was not restricted to the synagogue but was also employed in their everyday social interactions. The literary works of Philo of Alexandria and Josephus testify to the wider use of Greek language in the Roman Empire in the late first-century CE, throughout the Flavian dynasty and beyond.[70]

Besides language, assimilation to Roman culture could have happened to the Judeans through military conscription, and via the education system of the time. Josephus testifies to the fact that the Ptolemies settled large numbers of Egyptian Jews in Cyrenaica (modern-day Libya) as military colonists (Josephus, *Ag. Apion* 2.44). According to Williams, gymnasial education provided the means of assimilation to Greco-Roman culture by which people like Philo of Alexandria, Josephus, and Jews in the eastern part of the Empire derived deep knowledge of Greek literature and culture.[71] Other Jewish people may have been completely assimilated to Roman culture by adopting elite culture. One such person was Tiberius Julius Alexander, the nephew of Philo, the Jewish Philosopher about whom Josephus says:

> Then came Tiberius Alexander as successor to Fadus; he was the son of Alexander the Alabarch of Alexandria, which Alexander was a principal person among all his contemporaries, both for his family and wealth: he was also more eminent for his piety than this his son Alexander, for he did not continue in the religion of his country. (*AJ* 20.100)

Josephus's comment that Alexander Tiberius, who was procurator (governor) of Judaea under the emperor and prefect of Egypt under Nero, "did not continue in the religion of his country," indicates that Tiberius

---

70. Williams, "Jews and Jewish Communities," 316.
71. Williams, "Jews and Jewish Communities," 322.

abandoned Jewish monotheism to embrace Roman pantheism. It is also reflective of Tiberius's assimilation to Roman culture. Williams observes Josephus's comments as speaking "dispassionately of Tiberius Alexander's abandonment of his ancestral practices," comparing him unfavorably with his pious father, Alexander, one of the people that had successfully sustained Judean piety in the Diaspora.[72]

Slavery to a Gentile master was another one of the ways that facilitated Judean assimilation to Greco-Roman culture. Williams claims that "foreign captivity must have caused some Jews to abandon their ancestral ways. It is hard to see, for instance, how isolated [Judean] slaves with unsympathetic Gentile owners can have managed to obtain kosher foodstuffs or observe the commandment against working on the Sabbath."[73]

Consequently, what can be noted from this process of assimilation is that it was important for the Jews who assimilated to Roman culture to first undergo depersonalization. As a reminder, in the social sciences, depersonalization describes the process by which an individual categorizes themselves by subsuming the characterization of a group category to access an identity of deindividuated groups.[74] This is to say, while allowing one to maintain essential characterization of identity (such as ethnicity, racism, etc), depersonalization effects a process of socialization that enables the beholder to reconstruct a new social identity by embracing new norms, beliefs, and values that shape one's thinking and decision-making in society. As a result, the Judeans in Diaspora embraced new norms, beliefs, and values due to the cultural identity construction being offered in the Roman Empire. These norms, beliefs, and values were attached to the means of effecting assimilation such as language, military conscription and becoming a slave to a Gentile master. In this case, depersonalization as a process of effecting Jewish hybrid identity does not entail losing Judean ethnicity, but rather the suppression of certain indications of Judean cultural identity (such as language, dietary restrictions, rituals, etc.) in order to embrace a new culturally constructed hybrid identity that is more inclined towards Roman than Judean cultural identity.

This process of assimilation in effecting a hybrid identity entails the adoption of a new culturally constructed identity without losing some of the essential ethnic identity in order to become accepted in a new social

---

72. Williams, "Jews and Jewish Communities," 323.
73. Williams, "Jews and Jewish Communities," 302.
74. Esler, "Group Norms," 169; Kuecker, "Ethnicity and Social Identity," 71.

setting. However, it is a mistake to assume that the truth of Judean cultural hybrid identity in the Diaspora was that all the Judeans in the Diaspora ended up being assimilated into Roman Culture. There are some cases that suggest the opposite, as some Judeans strived to maintain of a more Judean cultural identity than a Roman one. This shall shortly be discussed when answering the question: how did the Jews who resisted assimilation to Roman culture manage to overcome the temptation to total assimilation and maintain more of a Judean than a Roman cultural identity?

4.2.3.3 Developing Hybrid Identity through Judean Tradition

Even before the destruction of the Jerusalem temple, Josephus tells us that Judeans felt that they needed to advocate for a maintenance of the source of their cultural identity. Noting the appeal of the Jews to Rome for the purposes of maintaining Judean religious laws while in Diaspora, Josephus says:

> But now, when Agrippa and Herod were in Ionia, a great multitude of Jews, who dwelt in their cities, came to them, and laying hold of the opportunity and the liberty now given them, laid before them the injuries which they suffered, while they were not permitted to use their own laws, but were compelled to prosecute their lawsuits, by the ill usage of the judges, upon their holy days, and were deprived of the money they used to lay up at Jerusalem, and were forced into the army, and upon such other offices as obliged them to spend their sacred money; from which burdens they always used to be freed by the Romans, who had still permitted them to live according to their own laws. (*AJ* 16.27–28)

Josephus reveals some concerns of the Judeans in the Diaspora regarding their ethnic cultural identity in the pre-70 CE period. In this case, Judeans are noted by Josephus as requesting Agrippa I (41–44 CE), King of Judaea, to petition for their grievances in Rome concerning the application of Judean law instead of that of the Romans to prosecute cases for Judeans in the Diaspora. The importance of Judean Law over Roman Law for the Diaspora Judeans is based on their belief that the former does justice to the distinctiveness of their cultural identity. Similar concerns for Judean ethnic cultural identity are noted by Josephus regarding the request by Diaspora

Judeans for Rome to grant them permission to send money to support the temple services in Jerusalem:

> Marcus Agrippa to the magistrates, senate, and people of Cyrene, sendeth greeting. The Jews of Cyrene have interceded with me for the performance of what Augustus sent orders about to Flavius, the then praetor of Libya, and to the other procurators of that province, that the sacred money may be sent to Jerusalem freely, as hath been their custom from their forefathers, they complaining that they are abused by certain informers, and under pretense of taxes which were not due, are hindered from sending them, which I command to be restored without any diminution or disturbance given to them. And if any of that sacred money in the cities be taken from their proper receivers, I further enjoin, that the same be exactly returned to the Jews in that place. (*AJ* 16.169–70)

The proposition here is that representation of a symbolic connection to monotheism provided the ideology that enabled post-70 CE Judeans in the Diaspora to maintain their cultural identity through identification with Israel. This identification enabled Judeans in the Diaspora to create a superordinate identity that was more of a Judean than Roman cultural identity that in turn enabled them to claim self-esteem for their community. Given the polytheistic environment in the Roman Empire, both of Josephus's comments here indicate how important Jerusalem was in maintaining the traditions of the Judeans in the Diaspora. In the aftermath of the destruction of the Second Temple in the late first-century, how did the Judeans in the Diaspora maintain their cultural identity? It is the task of the next section to answer this question, guided by the second premise of SRAT, supplemented by Scott's hidden scripts of resistance. In his book, *Domination and the Arts of Resistance*, James Scott outlines the resistance of a minority against the dominant group, claiming:

> It is plain enough thus far that the prudent subordinate will ordinarily conform by speech and gesture to what he knows is expected of him even if that conformity masks a quite different offstage opinion. What is not perhaps plain enough is that, in any established system of domination, it is not just a question of masking one's feelings and producing the correct speech acts and gestures in their place. Rather it is often a question of controlling what would be a natural impulse to rage, insult, anger, and the violence that such feelings prompt. There is no system of domination that does not produce its own routine harvest of insults and injury to human dignity-the

appropriation of labor, public humiliations, whippings, rapes, slaps, leers, contempt, ritual denigration, and so on.[75]

Scott suggests that when a subordinate group is violently treated by a dominating group, they employ non-violent response not only to suppress their anger and bitterness, but also to foster coexistence with the dominating group. Pre-70 Judean violent response to Rome's imperial policies earned an equal or even greater violent response from Rome, culminating in the destruction of the second Jerusalem temple. The post-70 Judeans in the Diaspora would likely have chosen a non-violent response to Rome in order to control what Scott calls "natural impulses to rage, insult, anger and violence that such feelings prompt."[76] Consequently, the interpretation of Judean first-century apocalyptic literature by Judeans contributed to the maintenance of Judean cultural identity in the Diaspora in the context of expressing non-violent resistance against Rome's domination. Thus, 2 Baruch (85.3–5) decrees of "YAHWEH the Mighty one and HIS Torah" represents the Torah as a political narrative for waging a divine war against Rome.[77] Not only does the concept "the Mighty One" represent the superiority of the God of the Diaspora Judeans over Jupiter, but politically it stands as a force superior to Roman imperial rule that inverts the Emperor's political power. The laments in 4 Ezra 10:21–23 (NRSV), that "our sanctuary has been laid waste . . . [to the effect that] Levites have gone into exile," and "our young men have been enslaved," resonate with Josephus's (*BJ* 7.96) comment that "Now Titus Caesar . . . removed, and exhibited magnificent shows in all those cities of Syria through which he went, and made use of the captive Jews as public instances of the destruction of that nation." Josephus, like 4 Ezra, recounts Titus's subjugation of Judaea in 70 CE, when vessels of the second Jerusalem temple were confiscated, and Judeans were taken into captivity by Rome.

Thus, although 4 Ezra most likely recalls the political domination of the Judeans during the Flavian dynasty, it is most certainly a political rhetoric of resistance against the Flavian dynasty. Consequently, 2 Baruch's (5.1) description of the sacking of the Jerusalem sanctuary by Titus as "haters . . . [who] will pollute YOUR Sanctuary," resonates with Scott's view of "hidden transcript" as a nonviolent response by a minority group against a dominant political one. In addition to the apocalyptic literature, further political

---

75. Scott, *Domination*, 36–37.
76. Scott, *Domination*, 37.
77. Citations from 2 Baruch are from the translation found in *Book 2 of Baruch*.

responses by the Judeans in the Diaspora are mirrored in the interpretation of the Torah. Because the Judeans regarded the Torah as having an eternal significance, even though the temple was destroyed, Judeans must have believed that the Law would continue to be applicable in the society, although perhaps in different linguistic forms. Thus, as a political tool that was intended not only to subvert Roman Law, but to preserve a Judean cultural identity, the Torah requirements on marriage prohibited intermarriage between Judeans and Gentiles (Gen 34:14; Deut 7:3–4). Faulkner observes that the prohibition on intermarriage with Gentiles, just like the insistence on the belief in monotheism and the food laws, implies that in the Diaspora this tenet of the Torah, although a conspicuous mark of Judean identity, exacerbated the isolation and marginalization of the Judeans.[78] In effect, this exclusive application of the Torah seems to have promulgated fixed boundaries of identity between members of Diaspora Judaism and outsiders. Esler concludes that 2 Baruch bears "the major theme of right and wrong cultic direction," and points to the application of cult and ritual alongside the Torah in first century Judaism to emphasize fixed boundaries of identity between the Judeans and outsiders.[79] The problem is that the Judeans, who followed Jesus as their messiah, like those of Matthew's community, had formed simultaneous movements.

Given the above exploration, it has been noted that in the late first-century CE, Torah interpretation was crucial for providing; (1) a political response against Rome's domination, (2) maintenance of communal norms of a Judean cultural identity, and, (3) establishing fixed boundaries of identity with outsiders. These functions of the Torah not only empowered the Judean communities in the Diaspora to resist Roman assimilation, but also provided a political narrative that attempted to maintain more of a Judean than Roman hydrid identity by symbolically connecting the Judeans in the Diaspora with the Law of their homeland, Judaea.

In addition to Torah interpretation, Sabbath observance had become a tool for expressing economic preference to maintain a Judean cultural identity in the Diaspora. In his *Embassy to Gaius*, Philo noted that during Emperor Gaius Julius Caesar's rule, whenever the distribution of food supplies in Rome coincided with the Sabbath, Judeans preferred to collect their grain supply a day later than compromise their observance of the Sabbath. Thus, Philo (*Embassy* 158) claims:

78. Faulkner, "Jewish Identity," 4–5.
79. Esler, "Rome," 28.

> Moreover, in the monthly divisions of the country, when the whole people receive money or corn in turn, he never allowed the Jews to fall short in their reception of this favour, but even if it happened that this distribution fell on the day of their sacred sabbath, on which day it is not lawful for them to receive anything, or to give anything, or in short to perform any of the ordinary duties of life, he charged the dispenser of these gifts, and gave him the most careful and special injunctions to make the distribution to the Jews on the day following, that they might not lose the effects of his common kindness.

From Philo's comment, the economic perspective of Diaspora Judaism can clearly be seen. Philo's comment poses a challenge which tests the allegiance of Diaspora Judeans to the Sabbath observance against economic benefits granted to them through the benefaction of either the emperor and/or Roman elites. The fact that the Judeans observed the Sabbath rather than accept imperial supplies of money and food is a silent act of resistance. It also indirectly demonstrates their monotheistic belief in God whom they regarded both as creator and provider of their needs such as food, as exemplified in the provision of manna to the Israelites while in the wilderness (Num 16:1–24). Here it is important to remember that the Books of Moses, or the Torah, form an important part of the religious texts of the Judeans beginning with the time of exile (c. 520 BCE). For those who believed in Jesus as their messiah, the time of the composition of Matthew's Gospel marked a shift in the importance of the Torah. Similarly, the demonstration of the importance of Jewish observance of the Sabbath was expressed by peoples' readiness to forfeit lawsuits when court appearances coincided with the Sabbath. Josephus (*AJ* 16.163) noted:

> [I]t seemed good to me and my counsellors, according to the sentence and oath of the people of Rome, that the Jews have liberty to make use of their own customs, according to the law of their forefathers, as they made use of them under Hyrcanus the high priest of the Almighty God; and that their sacred money be not touched, but be sent to Jerusalem, and that it be committed to the care of the receivers at Jerusalem; and that they be not obliged to go before any judge on the Sabbath day, nor on the day of the preparation to it, after the ninth hour.

By implication, insistence on observing the Sabbath instead of attending a court proceeding shows that Judeans gave precedence to their religious obligations over the legal requirement of Rome's judicial system, at least from the perspective of the Judeans in the Diaspora. Besides Sabbath observance, circumcision also formed an important source for Judean cultural identity in the Diaspora.

Just like the observance of the Sabbath, circumcision was an important religious ritual among Judeans that expressed political resistance to Rome, especially by Judeans in the Diaspora. Williams's comment that for Judeans, the rite of circumcision "was symbolic of their [Judean] covenant with God and hence their status as chosen people," indicates the political importance of the Judean observance of the rite of circumcision in the Diaspora.[80] Although Greeks and Romans viewed circumcision as barbaric and no different to castration, to the Judean circumcision defined the Diaspora Judeans in terms of Israel as God's own chosen nation.[81] It also symbolically connected them to fellow Judeans back at home in Judaea. To the Judeans, belonging to God's covenantal people, which was only accessible to Judeans, indicated an alternative to Roman citizenship. Josephus (*AJ* 6.1–18) speaks of the political significance of covenant whereby God fights against the Philistines on behalf of the Hebrews, the ancestors of the Judeans, to repossess the Ark of the Covenant from the Philistines. Thus, Judean rhetoric of covenant symbolized by circumcision was political in the sense that it expressed contestation of the Jewish people against Roman citizenship, particularly when this citizen was expected to be acquired through total assimilation to Roman culture. This non-violent resistance was important to Diaspora Judeans because it empowered them to maintain more of a Judean than Roman identity by contesting against assimilation to Roman culture. In other words, belonging to God's covenant, symbolized by circumcision, it contested Roman citizenship because it expressed one's more loyalty to Israel's covenantal traditions than to the Roman Empire.

The other Jewish Practice which had a more direct political and economic function is the Kaddish prayer:

> Exalted and sanctified is God's great name [Amen] in the world which He has created according to His will, and may He establish His kingdom in your lifetime and during your days, and within the life of the entire House of Israel, speedily and soon; and say, Amen. May His great Name be blessed forever and for all eternity. Blessed and praised, glorified and exalted, extolled and honored, elevated and lauded be the Name of the Holy One, blessed be He,

---

80. Williams, "Jews and Jewish Communities," 325.
81. Williams, "Jews and Jewish Communities," 325.

beyond all the blessings and hymns, praises and consolations that are spoken in the world; and say, Amen. May there be great peace from heaven, and life, for us and for all Israel; and say, Amen.[82]

According to Parsons, the Kaddish is an ancient prayer originally written in Aramaic. Kaddish in Hebrew, קדוש, literally means "sanctification," or "holiness." Parsons is emphatic about its political function because he says it expresses a petitioner's longing to establish God's Kingdom on earth. Parsons goes on to say that initially the Kaddish prayer was cited by the rabbis to conclude the sermon and later was developed and used for mourning. Developed over a long period of time, the Kaddish can be dated back to the second Jerusalem temple and continues to be recited by rabbis and modern Jews.[83] Thus, because of its connection to Judean traditional authorities such as the Jerusalem temple and rabbis, it was crucial in grounding Judean cultural identity in the Diaspora. The Kaddish Prayer may have been used by Diaspora Judeans in the first century CE.

The political function of the Kaddish prayer understood in the context of this book is that by mentioning "house of Israel" and "Israel," the prayer attempts to symbolically connect the petitioners to the God of Israel. It also underscores the religious and national traditional aspects of Israel to promote Judean monotheism against the hierarchical character of the Roman pantheon. By implication, invocation of the Kaddish prayer for Israel's God to establish his Kingdom on earth, assuring "great peace from heaven," denigrates the role of the *Pax Romana* in ensuring enduring peace and Roman political dominance in the world. Similarly, the "Name of the Holy One, blessed be He, beyond all the blessings," is a political expression with an economic dimension because it acknowledges the benefaction of God as "beyond all the blessing" which is granted either through the benefaction of the emperor or the Roman elites. Consequently, the Kaddish prayer bears a hidden political script that enforces resistance among the Diaspora Judeans in the Roman Empire to enforce and maintain cultural identity by symbolically identifying the community with Israel's God and Israel itself. Malina claims that in Antiquity "persons . . . define themselves almost exclusively in terms of the group in which they are embedded."[84] Consequently, the expression "for us and for all Israel," indicates that the

---

82. Cited in Parsons, "Reciting Kaddish."
83. Parsons, "Reciting Kaddish"; "Jewish Prayers."
84. Malina and Neyrey, *Portraits of Paul*, 158. See also "Jewish Prayers."

Kaddish prayer emphasizes a maintenance of group as opposed to individual identity among the Diaspora Judaeans.

The conception and practice of righteousness in the aftermath of the destruction of the second Jerusalem temple also significantly contributed to the maintenance of Judean cultural identity in the late first century CE. In the Greco-Roman cultural sense, righteousness denotes a customary or social standard. In the Judean sacred text (or Hebrew Bible, though the phrase is ambiguous since the LXX was a Greek version of the Hebrew Bible), it is reflective of the Judean perception of the quality of righteousness either directly derived from God, or from the behavior of the Israelites in obedience to covenantal obligations.[85] Thus, in Greco-Roman culture, the religious, economic and political freedom granted under acceptance and practice of Roman religion in the Empire provides the content of righteousness according to Roman socio-economic and political standards. Contrary to the Roman Empire, in first-century CE Judaism, as already discussed in the light of Torah, observance of the Sabbath, and circumcision, righteousness is more of a presentation or demonstration of lifestyle determined on account of one's Torah compliance than a mere social phenomenon. To Judeans, righteousness refers to a lifestyle that is manifested in the beholder's acts of mercy and a morality, reflective of God's gracious acts.[86] Due to the exclusive nature of observance of the

---

85. According to Silva, "δικαιοσύνη," 723, the concept of righteousness is derived from the Greek root word δίκη, which dates to the sixth century BCE and refers to custom, law, judgement, and punishment. Silva suggests that in the *Odyssey*, Homer used δίκη to refer to someone who is careful in observing accepted social customs, a reference which is in some ways equivalent to a civilized or moral person. Furthermore, Silva believes that Aristotle (*Politics*) understands δίκη to refer to the quality of a righteous person or standard. A judge is required to uphold justice in his judgment, that is; judicial justice, or a cardinal virtue. In the Greek reference, righteousness could occur as an abstract noun. In the Old Testament it does not simply refer to custom but expresses a covenantal relationship with Yahweh. For instance, in Exodus 23:7, Yahweh warns the Israelites not to kill the תַּהֲרֹג אֶל־וְצַדִּיק וְנָקִי רָשָׁע אַצְדִּיק לֹא־כִּי (do not kill the innocent and righteous for I will not justify the wicked). This shows that Yahweh's righteousness denotes the kind of justice he instructs the Israelites to uphold. Thus, in the Old Testament, divine righteousness is personified, for example, by the expression "the Lord loves righteousness and justice" in Psalm 33:5 in the LXX.

86. Jewish sectarian groups applied three categories of words to describe righteousness. These are: צְדָקָה, צֶדֶק, צַדִּיק. While צַדִּיק as witnessed by the Dead Sea Scrolls—for instance, 1QH 7.26–33; 1QH 4.38; 7.12—is an adjective referring to people who are properly religious, or one who lives by the covenant rules, and is also contrasted to the wicked—one who is rebellious against the covenant rules. Because צַדִּיק is absent in the 1QM, Przybylski thinks in this document—sons of light represents צַדִּיק to refer to

Torah, the Sabbath and circumcision, in the context of the absence of the temple and its cultic priesthood, in the post-70 CE, Judeans in the Diaspora contextualized Judean observance of righteousness to emphasize group cohesion and fixed boundaries of identity.

Consequently, to most Judeans in the Diaspora, righteousness had a political function because it was derived from God's gracious mercy. It was applied to the life of the Torah-complaint Jew, as opposed to a non-Torah compliant person or group. Of course, Torah non-compliant persons of the day would be those Judeans who had totally assimilated to the Roman culture, and who had allowed the polytheistic socio-economic and political values of the Empire to inform their lifestyle. In other words, Torah-conditioned righteousness as a cardinal marker of Jewish identity conditioned all political, religious, and economic engagements of the Judeans in the Diaspora. It is for this reason that the observance of kosher food, the Sabbath, and circumcision remained important to the Judeans in the Diaspora. Thus, practicing righteousness, for instance in the name of practicing circumcision, Sabbath observance, became a model for maintaining a Judean cultural identity in the Diaspora. In other words, all other categories of identity formation in Judaism, such as Sabbath observance, circumcision and Kaddish prayers, were primarily valued because they collectively participated in sustaining this Judean righteous life. Thus, righteousness is a cardinal marker of Diaspora Judean hybrid identity. Because righteousness was manifested through prayer and safeguarded through social interaction, it was effective in sustaining Judean resistant movements in response to Roman imperial policies.

Three factors related to oppressive political leadership are said to be responsible for the emergence of the Jewish resistance movements. In his monograph, *The Birth of Christianity: Discovering What Happened in the Year Immediately after the Execution of Jesus* (1998), John Dominic Crossan outlines a two-step theory that explains how the aristocracy in the first-century Roman empire subjugated the rights of peasants to impose their hegemonic power. Crossan refers to a traditional agrarian empire where the aristocracy took the agricultural surplus from the peasants, a system that consumed the agricultural industry and productivity of the peasants.

---

the—righteous ones. In Leviticus 7:15; 21:3, the noun צֶדֶק refers to righteous as a quality of life due to an act of mercy, which a person possesses because of performing a good deed. For instance, Moses was reckoned as צַדִּיק (righteous) for taking the bones of Joseph as they departed from Egypt to bury them in a valley (Exod 13:19). Przybylsk, *Righteousness in Matthew*, 32, 34.

He also refers to the aristocracy's engagement in commercializing of the agrarian empire, a system in which the aristocracy took the land itself from the peasants, and by doing so it obliterated the very identity and dignity of the peasants.[87] Crossan observes that this aristocratic system created a hegemonic power that perpetuated poverty among the peasants, because it converted the peasant from a scale freeholder to a tenant farmer to a day-laborer to a beggar or bandit.[88] Systematically, the aristocracy relegated the peasants to the group with the lowest social status in the Roman social strata. Second, alongside the peasants' resistance movement were the millennialists. The millennialists believed that the Roman Empire was an oppressive system, and this called for a cataclysmic event to end the oppressive structures and create a utopia which would replace the current oppressive system.[89] The oppressive system of the aristocracy denied the people basic rights, and thus not only marginalized them but also prompted them to become anxious and desperate for a renewed world order.

The *Assumption of Moses*, a first-century Palestinian Jewish writing, testifies to the existence of a millennial movement that may have been prompted by subjugation of peoples' rights by oppressive systems, such as the aristocracy:

> And then His Kingdom shall appear throughout all His creation, and then Satan shall be no more, . . . And the high mountains shall be made low, . . . And He will appear to punish the Gentiles, . . . And you will look on high to see your enemies in Ge(henna). (*As. Mos.* 10)

This text has eschatological undertones associated with themes such as the Kingdom of God that are found in the narrative of the Gospel of Matthew. Contrary to the Testament of Moses, the Gospel narrative emphasized missions to reach out to the Gentiles (Matt 28:19–20) rather than longing for their destruction.

The role of righteous, law compliance and promotion of Judean Messianic hopes had already been witnessed in the Psalms of Solomon, a mid-first century BCE Judean apocalyptic text:

> Wherefore sittest thou, O profane (man), in the council of the pious, seeing that thy heart is far removed from the Lord, Provoking

---

87. Crossan, Birth of Christianity, 157.
88. Crossan, Birth of Christianity, 158.
89. Duling, "Empire," 67–68.

with transgressions the God of Israel? Extravagant in speech, extravagant in outward seeming beyond all (men), Is he that is severe of speech in condemning sinners in judgement. And his hand is first upon him as (though he acted) in zeal, And (yet) he is himself guilty in respect of manifold sins and of wantonness.... Let God remove those that live in hypocrisy in the company of the pious, (Even) the life of such an one with corruption of his flesh and penury. (Ps. Sol. 4.1–6)[90]

The expressions "sittest ... in the council of the pious," and "may God remove from the devout," indicate that by evoking this first-century BCE Psalm, the Judeans in the Diaspora revealed the political role of the Judean conception of righteousness via reinforcing group cohesion in first century CE Judaism. Consequently, these two expressions reveal people's longing for God's intervention to deliver them from a Judean despotic leadership. Such Judean leadership was regarded as having profaned the name of God by departing from God's law. A Diaspora Judean reciting this Psalm might have had in mind in the late first century CE that the Jewish elite and aristocracy had colluded with the Roman officials to enforce Roman imperialism in Judaea. These Judean leaders may have been involved in facilitating the religious and political ideologies of the Roman emperor cult. Thus, they are collectively being described as "profane (man)" and their action as "Provoking with transgressions the God of Israel." This is reminiscent of the *fiscus Judaicus* (a post-73 CE temple tax) imposed on the Jews by Rome during the Flavian dynasty to support religious activities at Jupiter's temple at Capitoline in Rome. As already noted earlier, by practicing righteous activities such as almsgiving (צְדָקָה), not only were Judeans in the Diaspora demonstrating their belonging to God rather than to Jupiter or Zeus, but they were also politically expressing their non-violent resistance against Rome. Thus, although the Psalm of Solomon is a mid-first century BCE Jewish text, like the Torah, rhetorically it demonstrates the effectiveness of Jewish traditional religious norms and values in enforcing a political stance to preserve a Jewish identity both in Israel and in the Diaspora.

The above exploration of Jewish cultural traditions in facilitating the negotiation of Judean identity in the Diaspora in reference to the Roman assimilation has shown that the post-73 CE hybrid identity leaning more towards Judean cultural identity instead of totally succumbing to Roman assimilation was facilitated via Judean cultural practices. These Judean

---

90. Translation from Slick, "Psalms of Solomon."

cultural practices had the power to symbolically connect the Judeans in the Diaspora to ancient Israel's cultural practices including circumcision, Sabbath observance, purity regulations, and belief in monotheism. This observation prompts the question; given the option to either succumb to Roman assimilation or imitate Judean Diaspora resistance to Roman culture, how did the Jesus movement chose to respond during its emergence? To answer this question, the identity formation in the Jesus Movement in terms of its primary instigators, such as Paul, Peter, James, and John, will be considered. The importance of these individuals in this study is that they provided prototypical exemplars for their community on how to respond to Roman imperial policies.

4.2.4 Identity Construction and Maintenance in the Jesus Movement.

In the case of the Jesus Movement or early Christian communities, I speak of construction of identity because the Jesus Movement emerged in the mid-first century CE, as an offshoot of Judaism. Faulkner comments that the early Jesus movement began as a sect within Judaism. However, within a few decades of its origin (40–50 CE), it began to attract Gentiles to its communities, especially in the Diaspora."[91] Faulkner postulates that the Jesus Movement was not monolithic, but was a heterogeneous community consisting of several subgroups. The emergence and movement of the Jesus Movement has been explained as beginning in Galilee and spreading to Antioch through Jerusalem by scholars such as May and Meeks.[92]

Herbert May notes in his *Oxford Bible Atlas* the beginning of early Christianity in Jerusalem under the leadership of Peter and others (Acts 2–11). It soon spread as far as Antioch, the capital city of the Roman province of Syria. According to May, from Antioch early Christianity spread further eastward to Syrian-speaking Edessa. While making Antioch his center, Paul of Tarsus spread Christianity further west to the Roman province of Galatia to Rome, the headquarters of Roman Empire.[93]

In his article, "Breaking Away: New Testament Christianity's Separation from Jewish Communities," and grounding his views on Josephus, Meeks employs a social-science approach to reconstruct the emergence and

---

91. Faulkner, "Jewish Identity," 1.
92. See May, *Oxford Bible Atlas*; Meeks, "Breaking Away."
93. See May, *Oxford Bible Atlas*, 90–92.

spread of Apostolic Christianity from the Gospels of John, Matthew and Paul's letters. Meek asserts that John indicates that Christianity began as a Jewish sectarian community, because the followers of Jesus of Nazareth first worshipped in the Synagogues, and later after breaking with Judaism (John 9:22), continued in private homes. Moreover, Meeks observes that, unlike Johannine communities, which were first based on Synagogues, Pauline Christianity was primarily and characteristically a pluralism of "households." In other words, while Johannine sectarianism was based in Jewish Synagogues, Pauline communities were mostly situated within Christian movements.[94] Paul focused on building a "household of God" that united Jews and Gentiles, particularly as presented in Paul's letter to the Ephesians 2:11–12 although its Pauline authorship is contestable among New Testament scholars. Meeks thinks the Matthean community emerged from intra-sectarianism, that is; it was born out of conflict with its main opponents, who were the Pharisees and Scribes. Meeks claims that the Matthean community began as a Galilean Jewish sect, before the 66–73 CE revolt. After this revolt, the Matthean later joined existing Christian household communities at Antioch and interacted with both Jews in the Diaspora and Gentiles found there.[95] By taking this position on the emergence of the Matthean community from Galilee that finally settled in Antioch, Meeks illustrates why the narrative in the Gospel of Matthew (Matt 10:5–6; 28:19–20) shows such an interest with both Jews and Gentiles.

Although Meeks aptly depicts the emergence of Christianity in three categories, namely; Jewish Christianity (Matthean communities), Gentile Christianity (Pauline communities), and Hellenistic (Johannine Communities), he does not describe the strategies that were used to spread these three types of Christianity in the first century CE. McKnight in his monograph, *A Light among the Gentiles*, addresses this and explains how early Christians adopted the evangelistic approaches of proselytizing the Gentiles through "integration" and "resistance," as an approach for consolidating the communities of early Christianity.[96] It is noteworthy that Hann complements Meeks's theory of the emergence of early Christianity by providing some information about the Ebionites as part of the early Christian community. In his article "Undivided Way", Hann tells us that the Ebionites (Greek: the "Poor Ones") were a first-century CE Judeo-Christian community in

---

94. Meeks, "Breaking Away," 100–104.
95. Meeks, "Breaking Away," 113.
96. McKnight, *Light among the Gentiles*, 102–17.

Palestine and Asia Minor. Although the Ebionites regarded Jesus of Nazareth as the Messiah, they generally rejected his divinity. They also preferred the Epistle of James to the Pauline letters, and adopted two conflicting positions towards Mosaic Law; a pro and anti-Torah stance. On the one hand, there were anti-Jewish Ebionites who, while describing themselves as followers of Jesus of Nazareth, did not regard the Law of Moses as necessary for salvation and allowed fellowship with gentiles. On the other hand, there was a Jewish group who, though describing themselves as followers of Jesus of Nazareth, emphasized the necessity of Mosaic Law for salvation.

According to Hann, the Ebionites were a multi-ethnic community that included Jewish and Gentile converts but they were not part of the Gentile Church.[97] Could the pro-Jewish and pro-Gentile stance in the Gospel of Matthew be taken as a criterion to indicate that the Matthean community were indeed Ebionites? Consequently, the so-called Jesus Movement, or early Christian community, was a heterogeneous community comprised of people of Judean and Gentile origins. Understanding the Jesus Movement as a heterogeneous community is important not only because it allows for the tenets of the Social Rhetorical Analysis Theory to explain the relations between the Jesus Movement and Diaspora Judaism, but also because it provides the impetus for describing the role of Jesus in the communities addressed by Paul, James, John, and the first book of Peter. While Paul provides the example for Gentile Christianity's response to Rome and Diaspora Judaism, James, Peter and John provide that of Jewish Christianity.

4.2.4.1 Paul

The significance of Paul's writings, particularly his letter to the Romans, has been a matter of debate concerning the place of Paul in the Jesus Movement. This debate shows the evolution of Pauline studies, whereby early scholars argued that Paul addressed topics ranging from questions of human existence, to relations between Jews and Gentiles, and even Paul's connection with the Roman Empire. For instance, James Dunn regards the letters of Paul as revealing a multi-layered narrative theology that grapples with the "supreme questions of the reality and human existence."[98] This is especially exemplified in Paul's letter to the Romans.[99] Talbert claims that

---

97. Hann, "Undivided Way," 245–46.
98. Dunn, "Pharisees," 17–18.
99. Dunn, "Pharisees," 25.

Paul wrote his letter to the Romans to address a conflict caused by differences between the returning Jews exiled by Claudius and Gentiles in the city of Rome regarding their contrasting outlooks on the Mosaic Law in the Jesus Movement. The Jews returning from exile at the time of Nero had been expelled in 49 CE by Emperor Claudius for causing disturbances in the public order in Rome. According to Talbert, while the returning Jewish Christians preferred to keep some aspects of the Mosaic Law as part of their Christian faith, the Gentile Christians in Rome had developed some antipathy towards the Mosaic Law, seeing it as unnecessary for their Christian identity.[100] Talbert claims that Paul wrote the Romans in a call for unity by addressing the conflict caused by the difference in attitudes and views of the Gentile-Christians and Jewish-Christians. In line with Talbert's suggestion, Adeyemo contends that Paul wrote the letter to the Romans to "address problems in the church in Rome, including reconciling Jewish and Gentile believers and exhorting them to unity."[101]

A noticeable shift in Pauline studies is related to Paul's concerns regarding the Roman Empire, rather than Gentile-Jewish Christian relations in Rome. This shift has been expressed by Richard Horsley and Stanley E. Porter.[102] Their outlook contributes to the modern trend of connecting Paul with the Roman Empire. Grounding his argument on Paul's letter to the Romans and First and Second Corinthians, Porter argues that Paul replaces the reign of Caesar with that of Jesus. In First and Second Corinthians, Paul replaces the Roman hierarchy of obedience based on privilege with structures inaugurated by the instigation of the Lord Jesus Christ as the Son of God. Although this shift has the advantage of collectively presenting Paul's concern for amicable relations between Gentile and Jewish Christians and his concern for the place of Rome, the separation of Paul's interest with Judaism has the disadvantage of misrepresenting the trajectories of the relations that Paul was addressing in his letters. In his letters, particularly Rom 13:1–7 and 2 Corinthians 8, not only did Paul want to address the relations between Jewish and Gentile Christians, but he also wanted to produce a set of cultural norms, beliefs and values in order to empower his community to resist cultural assimilation by the Roman Empire and Judaization by Diaspora Judaism. Besides these two texts, in

---

100. Talbert, *Romans*, 6–8.

101. Adeyemo, *Africa Bible Commentary*, 1347.

102. Horsley, *Paul and Empire*; Horsley, *Paul and Politics*; Horsley, "Jesus-in-Movement"; Porter, "Paul Confronts Caesar," 192–93.

Romans 4 Paul argues that Gentiles could become heirs of Abraham, the father of Judean people, by trusting God as Abraham did. In his letter to the Galatians, Paul resisted the Judaizing Christianity that sought to make the Galatian Gentile Christians into law-abiding Christians.

Porter's analysis of Rom 13:1–7 provides helpful insights regarding the role of Paul's letter to the Romans in the construction, maintenance and the purpose of the narrative. Porter claims that Paul's letter to the Romans is reflective of two narratives: (1) the narrative of the emperor cult, emphasizing the divinity of the emperors and (2) a narrative constructed by Paul regarding Jesus as Son of God.[103] Before he juxtaposes these two narratives to show that the narrative in Romans is employed by Paul to replace the claims of divinity associated with the Roman emperor cult, Porter outlines calendrical inscriptions erected in Asia by Paulus Fabius Maximus, governor of Asia in 10/9 BCE. These calendrical inscriptions venerate the Roman emperors as god, son of god, creator, lord, and so forth, beginning from Julius Caesar to the time of Nero. Porter concludes that because these calendrical inscriptions were widely spread in Asia and in places Paul had travelled during his three missionary journeys, it follows that "Paul was very familiar with the wide-spread use of the terms that divinized the Caesars when he wrote his letter to the Romans."[104] Comparing Paul's narrative in Romans with the emperor cult narrative represented in the calendrical inscriptions, Porter concludes that Paul was "styling himself as the new erector of a new inscription to the true Lord Jesus Christ."[105]

Furthermore, Porter's analysis of Rom 13:1–7 presents the political aspects of the Jesus Movement as represented by Paul's thoughts in his letter to the Romans. Porter aptly observes that Romans 13:1–7 concerns two issues, namely; (1) taking the Roman authorities into account, and (2) imploring the Christians in the Roman empire to recognize the Lordship of Jesus Christ in a manner that does not necessarily result in unqualified obedience to Rome.[106] By implication, the political nature of Paul's rhetoric is based on the notion that Jesus's Lordship replaces the authority of the emperor in the Roman Empire. In other words, Paul displaces the political authority of the Emperor's with that of Jesus, the Son of God (Rom 1:3). A further political aspect of Paul's rhetoric in Romans 13:1–7

103. Porter, "Paul Confronts Caesar," 171–73.
104. Porter, "Paul Confronts Caesar," 173.
105. Porter, "Paul Confronts Caesar," 174.
106. Porter, "Paul Confronts Caesar," 186.

is emphasized by the semantic relationship of the phrase ὑποτασσέσθω (subject, or put into subjection, obedience) in Romans 13:1, discussed in the section that follows.

By regarding himself as a "slave of Christ" (Rom 1:1), calling for "obedience" (Rom 13:1) to a government which is from God, Paul rhetorically suggests that Christian obedience to earthly political authority is conditional on the fact that such an authority must be acceptable to God. Porter's claim, that in Romans 13:1–13 Paul calls for qualitative obedience, rather than positional authority, where qualitative authority refers to political authorities that are just in their conduct of business on earth, is useful for elaborating the political nature of Paul's rhetoric in Romans 13.[107] Paul was emphatic that Rome, as part of the political authorities of Paul's time, should only be obeyed not on all matters but when administering justice. According to Paul, this justice should be determined by Jesus's teaching. Thus, Paul's or his disciples' (Tertius in Rom 16:22) description of Jesus as "the Son who is the image of the invisible God" (Col 1:15) not only demonstrates the superiority of Jesus over and above the Roman emperors, but also his emphasis on the reliability of Jesus's teaching concerning justice as desired by God.

In Rom 13:1–7 Paul outlines the beliefs, norms, and values concerning the political obligations of the followers of Jesus to the Roman Empire. By positioning himself as a "slave of Jesus Christ" (Rom 1:1), Paul was engaging in political rhetoric to contest the authority of the emperor cult on behalf of Christians in Rome. Notably, contestation refers to "a social practice [that] entails objection to specific issues that matter to people" in authority.[108] Given that contestation "allows citizens to critically engage with the norms that govern them" it provides a "facilitative condition for citizens to obtain freedom from domination within a given society."[109] Because contestation is observed in "speech and language," rhetorically it can be inferred from written text, such as Paul's use of the phrase "slave of Jesus Christ" (Rom 1:1).[110] Thus, norms, beliefs, and values and the attendant non-violent political resistance outlined in Rom 13:1–7 in the literary context of Rom 1:1, were important in shaping the cultural identity of the Jesus Movement in the sense that they contributed to the construction

---

107. Porter, "Paul Confronts Caesar," 188–89.
108. Wiener, "*Theory of Contestation*," 112.
109. Wiener, "*Theory of Contestation*," 112.
110. Wiener, "*Theory of Contestation*," 112.

and maintenance of the cultural identity of Pauline communities that were part of the Jesus Movement.

If Paul's letter to the Romans provides an example of the political aspects of Pauline communities, then 2 Corinthians 8 illustrates the economic aspects of the Pauline communities during their emergence. In this context, Perkins's definition of economy is useful. He defines economy "as a range of activities to do with the production and supply of material needs and the careful management of the resources required to satisfy those needs."[111] Based on this definition, it is possible to see Paul's interest in involving the church in Corinth with contributing financially to alleviate poverty among the Judean Christians in Jerusalem (2 Cor 8) as an economic activity grounded in his conviction of Christian social values. Paul received financial contributions from the Christians in Macedonia, although they were a poor community (2 Cor 2:1–5). He then appeals to the Macedonian Christians by using the example of Christ sacrificing himself for the world (2 Cor 8:9). Like the Macedonians, Paul encouraged the Corinthian Christians to give financial support to the Jerusalem Church. This he did by saying to the Corinthians, "for you know the grace of our Lord Jesus Christ." With the view that Jesus was wealthy, "yet for your sake he became poor, so that you through his poverty might become rich" (2 Cor 8:9), Paul attempted to encourage the Corinthians to become interested in economic matters.

Two economic principles can be derived from Paul's concern for giving. First, by citing the Macedonian example, Paul wanted to lay down a belief system for the early church, emphasizing that for their economic survival, church members had to support one another. Second, by referring to Jesus, Paul suggests the beneficence of Jesus to his church. So, there is some economic narrative in 2 Corinthians 8 which is connected to the beneficence of Jesus Christ as the Jewish Messiah. Porter observes that there is a clear "hierarchy of beneficence" in 2 Corinthians 8:9, "one that begins with the Lord Jesus Christ and passes through Paul to the believers in Corinth and then to the believers in Jerusalem."[112]

Second Corinthians 8 shows that Paul engages in a nonviolent contestation of the economic system that kept the Emperor at the top and was mediated by the elites, with the local communities at the bottom. Thus, to the Jesus Movement, Paul pointed out that if they saw themselves as beneficiaries of Jesus Christ's grace, they in turn had the responsibility to become mutual

---

111. Perkins, "Power," 184.
112. Porter, "Paul Confronts Caesar," 192.

benefactors. Consequently, by outlining an economic beneficence system which was dependent on Christ's grace and not Rome's economic power, Paul provided a normative framework for the early Christian community, whose practicing in effect impacted on the maintenance of the cultural identity of the Jesus Movement in the first century CE. The more any Christian community practiced the type of beneficence system outlined in 2 Corinthians 8, the more they demonstrated their belonging to the Jesus Movement. Not only did Paul discuss the political and economic concerns for his community, but he also had in mind certain religious ideas, particularly about Diaspora Judaism. A religious aspect (though not separated from economic and political) of the Jesus Movement concerned the debate on whether first-century CE Christianity and Judaism had yet parted ways.

In his monograph, *The Conflict of the Church and Synagogue*, James Parkes's discussion regards the parting of ways as a reference to the social separation of Christianity from Judaism. James Dunn, in his monograph, *Jews and Christians: The Parting of the Ways*, suggests that parting of the ways involved the social separation between the Jews and Christians, particularly how and when Christological claims made social separation between Judaism and Christianity inevitable.[113] In his article, "The Ways That Parted: Jews, Christians, and Jewish-Christians ca 100–150 CE," Shaye C. Cohen discusses two issues regarding the parting of the ways. Cohen is of the view that in the second-century CE, Gentiles, Jews (both who did not believe in Christ) and Christians (Gentiles who believed in Christ) constituted separate communities, each with its own identity, rituals, institutions, authority-figures and literature. Cohen also says that by around 100 CE, Christian communities were distinct from Jewish, not only on account of the Hebrew writings of sages of Roman Palestine, but also on account of the evidence provided by the Greek-writing Jewish communities of the Diaspora.[114]

In view of the debate regarding the parting of the ways between Jews and Christians, Paul's letter to the Romans and 2 Corinthians 8, supports the argument that in the mid-first century CE, Gentiles had joined Jewish Christian communities, particularly in Antioch. This is based on information in Gal 2:12–17. The movement to Antioch probably necessitated separation of Judean believers in Christ from Judeans (who did not believe in Christ). Although this separation between Jewish-Christians

---

113. Dunn, *Jews and Christians*, 368.
114. Cohen, "The Ways That Parted," 30–31.

and Judeans was probably due to the understanding of Jesus Christ as the Messiah. This was more of a religious than merely a social separation, because during the last half of the first-century CE, Judeans and Jewish-Christians were still socially integrating in the Diaspora, for instance; in Rome, Alexandria and Syrian Antioch.

When Paul's description of himself as δοῦλος Ἰησοῦ χριστου (slave of Jesus Christ) in Rom 1:1 is viewed in the context of his conversion to Christianity, in which he still values the Torah (Rom 7:12–16) and the figure of Abraham (Rom 4:1–3), it shows that Paul deliberately wrote his letter to the Roman Christians in order to point out the rootedness of Christianity in Judaism because the Torah and the figure of Abraham are such important markers of Judean identity, hailing back to Israel's covenant with God (Gen 17:1–27; Exod 20:1–26; Jer 34:8–22). Paul approached the issue of Abraham and the Torah from the point of view of their role in directing the audience to Jesus. By doing so, he was at the same time constructing a Christian cultural identity for the Jewish Christians in Rome. At that time, the Judeans in Rome were mainly Judeans in an ethnic sense. Those who had accepted the belief that the Messiah had come in the form of Jesus, for example Priscilla and Aquila (Acts 18:2–3), seemed to belong to a distinct form of Judaism. Thus, early Christianity (the Jesus Movement) was first a form of Judaism. The reason for this is elaborated in Rom 4, when Paul attempts to show that Gentiles, through trust in God, were offspring of Abraham. In other words, Judeans who accepted Jesus as Messiah had acquired a superordinate identity; their acceptance of Jesus as Messiah entailed transition to a complex identity that, although essentially shaped by cultural norms, beliefs, and values of the Jesus Movement, at the same time it encompassed Judean ethnic identity. Essentially, belief in Jesus the Christ was added to their Jewishness.

Furthermore, on account of Rome's official grant to the Judeans of the right to practice their monotheistic religion, this meant that both Judeans and Jewish Christians, who were all ethnic Judeans because of their connection to Judaism, Rome classified them as one community in specific localities. For instance; in Rome, Antioch, Alexandria, etc, they were Jewish communities. Although Jewish Christians were socially integrated with other Judeans who did not believe in Jesus as the Messiah, in terms of religious practice, they were two different groups. Jewish Christians were practicing a kind of Judaism that focused on accepting Jesus as the Messiah, and not Judaism grounded only in Israel's ancient cultural traditions.

Ideally, the superordinate identity of Judean culture should have enforced social cohesion among the Judeans in the Diaspora despite their differences in attitude regarding acceptance of Jesus as a Messiah.

It is noteworthy that Paul views the churches in Macedonia as endowed with God's grace, even though he claimed that they were living in "extreme poverty." He still recommended they contribute financially to support the Jerusalem church, saying that they "gave as much as they were able, and even beyond their ability" (2 Cor 8:8–13). Here again the role of a superordinate identity within the Jesus Movement is apparently contributing to the social integration between a mostly Gentile Christian congregation of Macedonia, and a mostly Judean Apostolic church in Jerusalem. In terms of ethnic composition, these two Christian congregations were different, also separated by a significant distance. From a religious perspective, particularly in reference to their Christian identity, they are symbolically united by their gift of thanks for the financial support from the Macedonian churches. The same support was probably received by Judean Christian communities in Jerusalem. Thus, this act of giving performed the religious role of re-enforcing social cooperation between Gentile and Jewish Christians in the Jesus Movement. This financial support underpinned a normative framework for social support among its members. This in turn became an important way of maintaining a common Christian cultural identity in Antiquity, despite the distance that separated the early Christian communities.

Having looked at Pauline communities as sources of cultural identity in the Jesus Movement, the other communities that constituted the Jesus Movement will also be analyzed. This analysis is limited to the congregations addressed by James, Peter and John. While James provides economic examples, Peter and John provide examples for the social and political dimensions of the Jesus Movement.

THE SOCIAL SETTING

4.2.4.2 Other Early Communities in the Jesus Movement: James, Peter, and John

Several debates surround the best approach for reading the letter of James.[115] Westfall analyzes James from an economic perspective.[116] She regards James to be a critic of the rich and advocate of the poor against the local Jewish elite. James also denounces exploitation by the Roman Empire. In her analysis of the varied responses of early Christian communities (that is, the Jesus Movement) to the Roman Empire, Westfall is guided by three sets of questions: First, what is the author's intention? Did the author intend to interact with the Roman Empire either by accommodating or confronting what was written? Second, what is the perception of the audience? Would the recipients read a given passage or phrase as a negotiation or confrontation of Empire? Third, what is the relationship to the Roman authorities? Would they perceive a passage or phrase as offending their authority, or consider it subversive to the Empire?[117] Westfall's method is pertinent in interpreting the discourse of the Jesus Movement not only because it helps to provide an understanding of the effect of the implied author on two audiences—the church readers of the text and the Roman authorities—but it can also help to conceive the fact that every given text has at least three layers of meaning; authorial intention, immediate audience, and the larger audience-conditioned meaning. With this approach in mind, the function of the authorship of James, Peter and John (in the Book of Revelation) in shaping the cultural identity of parts of the early Jesus Movement will be explored.

James begins by pointing out the deplorable economic conditions of the people in the local communities in comparison to the rich elites in the Roman imperial social strata. The people mentioned by James belong to the lowest rung of the social ladder, classifying them as "poor men in filthy clothes," and as brothers or sisters without clothes or daily food (Jas 2:2, 15). The exploitation of the poor by the rich is characterized by the denial of

---

115. See, for instance, John Painter. He regards James as one who epitomized righteousness and justice and one who mediated between Paul and the Jewish Christians who opposed Paul (Painter, *Just James*, 1, 8). Elsa Tamaz, reading James from a liberation theology perspective, understands it as a subversive discourse attacking the exploitative landowners and the carefree life of the merchants in James 5:1–6 and 4:13–17 (Tamaz, *Scandalous Message of James*, 1).

116. Westfall, "Running the Gamut," 231.

117. Westfall, "Running the Gamut," 230.

wages to poor farm workers after they mowed and harvested the fields of the rich landowners, and the condemnation and murder of the poor by the rich (Jas 5:4, 6). Thus, in 4:13–17 and 5:1–6, James addresses the arrogance of the perpetrators of unjust treatment of poor local communities. Westfall claims that in 4:13–17 and 5:1–6, James addresses merchants and wealthy landowners in the Roman Empire. Moreover, in James (2:6), the author noted the failure of the judicial system to defend the plight of the poor when the rich dragged them to court.[118] Verse 2 according to Westfall "[James] depicts a corruption of the Jewish courts by the Roman practice, presumably through the collusion of the local elites."[119] Given the above exploration, it can be argued that James wrote his letter to contest exploitation in the Roman Empire by the elites and Jewish aristocracy. This contestation is important in shaping the cultural identity of the Jesus Movement, as it outlines a belief system which encourages adherents to adopt a stance of non-violence to fight economic injustice, perceived as exploitation, by the readers of the letter. Thus, the Roman Empire most likely would have perceived the Letter of James as promoting confrontation against economic systems operational in the Empire. Thus, James should not be understood as anti-Pauline as suggested by some scholars, but rather supplementary to Paul due to his emphasis on non-violent confrontation against injustice and exploitation as aspects that ought to accompany faith in Jesus Christ.

The significance of 1 Peter to the early Christian community is debated among New Testament scholars. Views range from seeing 1 Peter's principal concern to be redemption, to a response to Rome's colonizing presence, to identity formation.[120] 1 Peter also represents a reflection of the early Christian economic situation. The author of 1 Peter outlines three issues that seem to be sources of suffering for Christians: (1) rejection and public disgrace (1 Pet 3:8—4:19); (2) harsh treatment of slaves (1 Pet 2:18–25); and (3) vulnerability of women and threats towards their marital status (1 Pet 3:1–17). To address these anomalies, Peter advocates

---

118. Westfall, "Running the Gamut," 234.

119. Westfall, "Running the Gamut," 235.

120. Mason and Martin, *Reading 1–2 Peter and Jude*, 9, argue that Clement of Alexandria and Didymus of Alexandria understood 1 Peter to be a letter about redemption, conversion, and its consequences. Joel B. Green, *1 Peter*, 1, claims that the letter was written to address Rome concerning its sanctioned religion and its imperial, colonizing presence and practices. Paul Trebilco, *Outsider Designations*, 80–81, regards 1 Peter's functionally as a tool for identity formation in early Christianity by differentiating the believers in Christ from those standing outside Christ.

first that slaves submit to their masters in order to model Christ-like suffering to the community at large, and to seek God's favor when accepting this suffering (1 Pet 2:18–25). Second, women are to submit to their husbands in order to win favor with Christ (1 Pet 3:1–6). This kind of submission, which is connected to Christ's submission, had some purpose in depicting Christ to the larger community. Westfall says that in a culture where women were despised for being fearful, men were honored for being courageous. Slaves were denigrated by virtue of being slaves. Thus, the culture implored women and slaves to be submissive to their husbands and masters, respectively. Consequently, according to Westfall, Peter's language "reversed the honor-shame language in such a way that he has shown that women in the Christian communities are to be the social peers of men."[121] Essentially, Peter employed a non-violent approach to contest the social honor-shame value system in the Roman Empire.

Honor and shame were dependent not on the Roman imperial expectation, but on Jesus's tradition. This is supported by Jesus's saying "whoever wants to become great among you must be your servant" (Matt 20:26 NIV). This contested Rome's social values of honor and shame, which in turn provides a normative framework for Christians based on the value of honor. 1 Peter provides the Jesus Movement yet with another means of maintaining their Christian cultural identity by contesting the social honor-shame continuum of the Roman Empire. While James and Peter provided the criteria for economic and social responses, John's Revelation is a political response to the Roman Empire.

The Book of Revelation, attributed to an otherwise unspecified author, is said to have been written towards the end of the first-century CE.[122] It mirrors the political reign of the Flavian dynasty, particularly the political tenure of Domitian (81–96 CE). Like the book of Daniel, the Book of Revelation belongs to the apocalyptic *genre* and so it communicates its message through symbolism and imagery. The problem being addressed in the Book of Revelation, according to Westfall, is that of Jewish Christianity which is "caught in the crossfire of hostility from Judeans, the official actions and policies of the Roman empire towards both Christians and Judeans, and unofficial public hostility."[123] Consequently, Revelation shows

---

121. Westfall, "Running the Gamut," 243.

122. Adeyemo, *Africa Bible Commentary*, 1543–44; Westfall, "Running the Gamut," 251.

123. Westfall, "Running the Gamut," 251.

serious concern for seven churches that are symbolically represented under pressure from a myriad of challenges, ranging from poverty (Rev 2:8–9), to materialism (Rev 3:17–18), attacks through slander, rejections, persecution, imprisonment, martyrdom (Rev 2:9–10, 13) to idolatry (Rev 2:14, 20) and sexual immorality (Rev 2:14, 20–23). Westfall claims that the issues outlined in Revelation are addressed through prophecies that predict the future destruction of the Roman Empire, and the victory and sovereignty of God and Christ.[124] Westfall's suggestion creates the impression that Revelation infers Rome's enmity against Christians. Thompson contends that the language of the narrator indicates an "attitude towards Judaism rather than Jewish actions against Christians." Its audience is part of Roman society "as a group of people who understood themselves as a minority that continuously encounters and attacks the Christian community and even larger Roman social order."[125] Thus, given Westfall and Thompson's views, Revelation functions as an apocalyptic narrative, and a reflection of the a Jewish-Christian narrator's contesting Rome's socioeconomic and political activities such as emperor worship and other perceived forms of injustice emanating from Rome to common person.

From Revelation 6:1 to 8:1, God responds to this injustice with a series of destructive acts, symbolically communicated through seven seals; earthquake, fire, plague, famine, conflict, and violence. All these events have the risen Christ as the commander of the army of destruction. Eventually, ultimate defeat of Babylon happens: "with a mighty voice the angel shouted: Fallen! Fallen is Babylon the Great!' She has become a dwelling for demons and a haunt for every impure spirit, a haunt for every unclean bird, a haunt for every unclean and detestable animal" (Rev 18:2 NIV). When comparing Revelation 18 to 21:24 (concerning honoring of the city by the Kings of the earth), Fiorenza claims that the author of Revelation "contrasts the splendor and power of the Roman empire with that of the empire of God and Christ . . . to encourage readers to resist the murderous power of Rome."[126]

Ideologically, the symbolic imagery of the risen Christ as the commander at the helm of the defeat of Babylon was probably politically understood by Roman authorities as a subversive rhetoric intending to overthrow Rome's political influence in the Empire and replace it with a political figure represented by Jesus Christ as the Jewish Messiah. Consequently, to the Johannine

124. Westfall, "Running the Gamut," 253.
125. Thompson, *Revelation*, 174, 195.
126. Fiorenza, "Rhetoricity," 267.

audience, Revelation symbolically communicates the victory of the Jesus Movement over the prevalence of Rome's political ideology and its influence in the Empire. To this end, David Barr observed that reading the visions of Revelation 12–13 together with the traditions of the combat myths about Python and Seth-Typhon and the claim for divine status for the emperor, who is also considered a personification of the dragon's opponent, would imply the utter deconstruction of this Roman imperial ideology.[127]

By focusing on the risen Christ as the head of the army that eventually defeats Babylon the Great, John outlines a belief system for his communities that formed part of the Jesus Movement. Jesus in this system was regarded as the Jewish Messiah, which ideologically also set a tradition that regarded him as a politically authoritative figure that overcame the evil in Roman society. The belief outlined by John crystalizes the norm among the Jewish Christians to regard Jesus as the ultimate righteous one who has the power to overcome all political enemies of the Judean people. This belief and its attendant norms are thus important in the construction of the cultural identity of the Jesus Movement, because they provide instructions for political engagement.

4.3 Conclusion

How was identity shaped in Antiquity? Rome seems to have set the pace for identity formation among both Diaspora Judeans and adherents of the Jesus Movement. Just as Rome's imperial system was multivalent in nature in the formation of cultural identity, so was the response from Diaspora Judeans and the Jesus Movement. While this multivalent response was important for enforcing resistance against Rome for the maintenance of the hybrid identity of the Judeans in Diaspora, to the Jesus Movement it provided the impetus for contesting Rome's ideology in order to construct and maintain a distinct Christian cultural identity. This complex process of identity-formation prompts the following question: given the path of identity formation pursued by the Roman Empire, Diaspora Judaism and the Jesus Movement, how did the Matthean community negotiate their cultural identity during their emergence in late first century CE? The next chapter answers this question.

127. Barr, "The Lamb," 201. In his work on the symbolic transformation of the world in Revelation, Barr inverts Rome's political power by making the oppressed Christians the winners and the Roman authorities the losers.

CHAPTER 5

MATTHEW 6:9–13 AND CONSTRUCTION OF IDENTITY POLITICS

IN THE CONTEXT OF the Roman imperial assimilation program, the emergence of the Jesus Movement, and the maintenance of Judean hybrid identity in the Diaspora, how does Matthew employ his version of the Lord's Prayer to construct the identity politics for his community? To answer this question, we shall investigate the social, cultural and historical significance of Matthew's version of the Lord's Prayer before exploring its rhetorical function in constructing identity politics for the community of Matthew.

5.1 Cultural, Social, and Historical Perspectives

In this exploration, Robbins's social, cultural and historical inter textures, which collectively constitute the tenets for inter texture, are instructive.

5.1.1 Cultural Perspective

Cultural inter texture employs reference, echoes and comparisons to contribute to socio-rhetorical interpretation.[1] Consequently, the Lord's Prayer

---

1. In socio-rhetorical interpretation, "culture" refers to "the status of a phenomenon that appears in a wide range of literature that spans many centuries" (Robbins, *Tapestry*, 110). This is in reference to a person's or peoples' traditions. Robbins's definition of culture implies that culture refers to a group's shared meaning derived from traditionally inherited beliefs, norms and values of a given community. Thus, cultural inter-texture is the focus of an inter-textual analysis that crosses the boundaries of the Biblical canon to include Greco-Roman, Hebraic, or Jewish cultural intertexture. Robbins, *Exploring*,

in Matthew's Gospel echoes the Aramaic Kaddish prayer. This means that it depicts some cultural inter textuality with this Jewish prayer. In its literary perspective, the Kaddish prayer declares:

> Exalted and sanctified is God's great name (Amen) in the world which He has created according to His will, and may He establish His Kingdom in your lifetime and during your days, and within the life of the entire House of Israel, speedily and soon; and say, Amen. May His Name be blessed forever and for all eternity.[2]

According to John J. Parsons, the Kaddish Prayer is part of the Jewish liturgical tradition that was originally recited in the synagogue. It was later devoted to funeral events as a prayer addressing the mourners. But like Matthew's version of the Lord's Prayer, Parsons suggests that the Kaddish Prayer is "an ancient Jewish prayer" whose main intention was "to express a longing for the establishment of God's Kingdom on earth."[3] Evans, grounding his argument on linguistic function, contends that Matthew's version of the Lord's Prayer depicts a more interactive picture of God because it refers to God in the second person, unlike the Kaddish Prayer that refers to God in third person.[4] However, the Kaddish Prayer was intended to address mourners. The third person singular reference to God in the Kaddish Prayer makes sense in a mourning context because the speaker, being a Judean who avoided direct mention of God's name, probably intended to speak indirectly about God and more directly to the mourners. Thus, Parsons observes that the Kaddish Prayer was recited to a mourner in the presence of a quorum, or a congregation of ten or more male adults, rather than to God. The prayer was originally recited in Hebrew and later practiced in the Christian community (Luke 11:2–4) before Matthew adopted it for his community use. Grelot suggests that from the point of view of the opening, "our Father" (Matt 6:9), Matthew's Lord's Prayer is influenced by "*semitismes qui s'y rencontrent et celle du cadre culturel dans lequel la predication evangelique fut effectuee.*"[5] Thus, Grelot suggests that Matthew probably valued the prayer because it grounds the intra-cultural identity of the Matthean community in earlier Judean liturgical traditions.

62–63; Robbins, *Tapestry*, 110.
  2. Cited in Parsons, "Reciting Kaddish."
  3. Parsons, "Reciting Kaddish."
  4. Evans and Zacharias, *What Does Scripture Say?*, 145–46.
  5. Grelot, "La Quatrième Demande," 299.

Besides the Jewish Kaddish Prayer, Matthew's Lord's Prayer echoes Greco-Roman cultural practices of prayer. For instance, in his *Iliad* (3.320–25), Homer portrays human beings evoking Jupiter as "Father who rules from Ida's height . . . most great glorious." Although similarities between Matthew's version of the Lord's Prayer and Jewish and Greco-Roman prayers from linguistic point of view can be noted, there is some difference. The main difference between Matthew's Lord's Prayer and the Kaddish Prayer is not only based on second-person reference to God, but also that Matthew's narrative acknowledges Jesus as *Imma-nu-el*. That is, "God with us" (Matt 1:23), a reference which provides intra-cultural and a continual reference to God in Judean and various local communities in the Roman Empire, respectively.

It is noted above that in composing the Lord's Prayer, Matthew alluded to Greco-Roman and Jewish cultural aspects of prayers to reveal his community's awareness of their existence. In other words, Matthew's allusion here probably reveals something about his audience's knowledge of the literary-cultural practices that was going on in the Roman Empire.

5.1.2 Social Perspective

To achieve social intertexture, according to Robbins, interpreters usually focus on analyzing conventional practices, customs, and traditions that "support conventional practices in certain kinds of social settings."[6] Unlike cultural knowledge which is limited to specific groups and has to be taught under careful use of language, social knowledge is readily accessible to all people through general interaction. Generally, social knowledge is constituted from the following four categories; social role (e.g., soldier, shepherd, slave), social institutions (e.g., empire, synagogue, traders' association), social codes (e.g., honor, hospitality), and social relationships (e.g., patron, friend, enemy, kin). Thus, social inter texture aims to address social meaning that interpreters investigate using data outside the text such as archeological data, meaning of identities, texts, institutions, etc.[7] Thus, social inter texture enables the interpreter of a Biblical text to access a wide range of social facts that may have influenced the discourse of the early Christian communities, because early Christian communities were not insulated from society but actively participated in the first century

---

6. Robbins, *Tapestry*, 116.
7. Robbins, *Exploring*, 62–63; Robbins, *Tapestry*, 118–20.

social world of the Mediterranean. Jupiter was regarded as the Supreme Patriarch and ruler of the cosmos, similar to the Roman emperor, who was also acknowledged as "Father of the Roman state."

Although Keener claims that in his understanding of God as "Father," Jesus was most likely influenced by early Judaism and the Hebrew Bible rather than Greek language,[8] the social influence of the Greco-Roman cultural phenomenon on the Lucan perspective of God as "Father" should not be discounted (Luke 11:2). This suggests two scenarios. First, in his version of the Lord's Prayer, Matthew probably decided to redact Q's version of the Lord's prayer by adding the personal pronoun "our" to refer to God as "our Father" (Matt 6:9), in order to give the prayer a Jewish, rather than a Greco-Roman liturgical flavor, thereby strengthening the intra-cultural identity of the Matthean community. This was to emphasize more of the Judean aspect of the cultural identity of the Matthean community. The second scenario relates to the effect of Matthew's redaction. By adding the pronoun ἡμῶν, the narrative makes indirect reference to the audience, because Jesus's speech in the Lord's Prayer presupposes that Matthew's audience, rather than Jesus's disciples, are the ones being addressed.

Furthermore, Robbins's social inter texture helps us to explore how Matthew's version of the Lord's Prayer portrays some social relations. For instance, in Homer's *Odyssey* (1.2) and in Virgil's *Aeneid* (1.65; 2.648; 10.2), Jupiter/Zeus is recognized as "Father . . . king of kings," and "Father of gods and King of men," respectively. This recognition of the Greco-Roman principal deity had some social implications in the Roman Empire. The understanding of Jupiter as "Father" and "King" became the grounds for granting social honor and power to the Roman emperors. Thus, rhetorically the narrator's indirect reference to the pronoun "our Father" in Matt 6:9 reveals the narrator's intentions to sensitize his community of their belonging to God rather than to Jupiter. This means, Matthew's Lord's Prayer critically alludes to Greco-Roman social values of honor, particularly derived from Roman principle deity, Jupiter, which in turn enforced Roman citizenship and allegiance to the emperor.

5.1.3 Historical Perspective

Unlike the social inter texture which focuses on social practices that occurred regularly as life events, the historical inter texture refers to

---

8. Keener, *Gospel of Matthew*, 217.

experiences and events concurrent with the composition of a Biblical text. For instance, John 9:22, 12:42, and 16:2, seem to show a historical event occurring in the early Christian community in the post-70 CE period. This is not an attempt to undermine the Martyn-Bauckham Johannine community hypothesis controversy regarding the historical function of John's Gospel. Rather, it is to dispute Bauckham's view (regarding the text as addressing general audiences, not specific groups) which gives preference to J. Louis Martyn's position by supporting Wally V. Cirafesi's hypothesis on the linguistic functions of the Gospel of John that "allows for the reconsideration of traditional perspectives on issues such as the authorship, audience and historical value of John's Gospel."[9] Although Cirafesi's view that John "allows for the reconsideration of traditional perspectives on issues such as the authorship, audience and historical value of John's Gospel", implies that ἀποσυνάγωγος in John 9:22, 12:42, 16:2 is reflective of a historical account, it neither supports total separation between the Matthean community with post-70 CE Judaism, nor does it discount the possibility of the text's rhetorical power and persuasion. In other words, ἀποσυνάγωγος in John 9, 12 and 16, like μαστιγόω in Matthew 10:17, may not reflect an actual historical circumstance but may be trying to shape the readers' perceptions by the use of rhetoric that may create its own reality rather than reflect it. What does Matthew's Lord's Prayer have to do with inter texture? At several points, Matthew's Lord's Prayer provides references that reflect on the events associated with Rome's power.

Carter suggests that the petition phrased "your kingdom come" (Matt 6:10) refers to the establishment of "God's empire as life giving, not as oppressive . . . to exercise authority over the Kingdom of the world . . . including the Roman Empire."[10] Carter explicitly shows that Matthew's Lord's Prayer indirectly mirrors the power relations of the Matthean community in the Roman Empire in first-century CE. In this relationship, the Matthean community was probably experiencing some oppression by living under the socio-economic elites in the Roman Empire. Thus, Matthew's narrative reflects Jesus's arrest and harsh treatment by the early collaborators of the first-century Roman Empire, namely; Caiaphas, the high priest, and his security guards (Matt 26:3, 57–62). In this case, rhetorically the narrative intends to communicate a continuity of similar oppression

---

9. Cirafesi, "Johannine Community," 173. See also Martyn, *History & Theology*, 26–30.

10. Carter, *Matthew and the Margins*, 165.

MATTHEW 6:9–13 AND CONSTRUCTION OF IDENTITY POLITICS

of the Matthean community in Syria in the late first-century CE by the Roman elites. Suetonius (*Dom.* 13.2) confirms that in the period 81–96 CE Domitian, the younger brother of Titus, asserted his oppressive rule by demanding the Roman citizens to address him as "our Lord and god." However, Suetonius was writing in the post-Domitian era, which marked the end of the Flavian dynasty. At the time of his writing, he was hired as an Orator by Trajan. As such, his testimony may not be authentic and reliable. However, Matthew's insistence on forgiveness of debts (Matt 6:12) reflects a late first-century application of the *prosbul*, which was intended to invert liberty from debt on account of the Jubilee covenantal decrees (Deut 15:1–3; Lev 25), and so draw attention to the unjust treatment of the poor by the wealthy in the society. Keener rightly observes that in the Gospel narrative of Matthew, 'debt' could mean more than economic debt, it could also include sins.[11] Thus, the historical inter texture of Matthew's Lord's prayer, on account of its emphasis on God's Kingdom to come and forgiveness of debts, reveals that Matthew borrows from Hebrew traditions to contest Jewish aristocratic elites' application of the *prosbul* to alleviate social oppression in the Matthean community.

Although Robbins's intertexture helps us to reflect from Matthew's version of the Lord's Prayer Jewish liturgical traditions, Roman social values, particular, shame-honor values, and glean some historical injustices contemporaneous to the time of the writing of the Gospels. For instance, the imposition of the *prosbul* by Judean aristocracy, Robbins's tenets of intertexture falls short of showing how Matthew employs his version of the Lord's Prayer to constructs the identity politics for his community, an issue hinted by the recent research of Baasland and Du Toit but is yet to be clarified, particularly by the use of the concepts of recategorization, depersonalization, identification, contestation and legitimation. These concepts play a crucial task in this chapter because they form the backbone of our definition of identity politics, namely, *borrowing and accommodation of beliefs, values and norms of an ancient traditional community by a marginal group to reconstruct their identity through recategorization, identification and contestation in order to overcome domination by a majority group and achieve the goal of encouraging non-violent attitude, advocate social good and promote an inclusive household.*

---

11. Keener, *Gospel of Matthew*, 233.

5.2 Reconstruction and Legitimation of a Christian Identity

Baasland and Du Toit show that Matthew's version of the Lord's Prayer played a significant role in shaping the identity of the Matthean community.

5.2.1 Baasland

Baasland noted that the content of the Matthean Lord's Prayer elaborates the concept of righteousness in terms of character formation. He claims that the immediate literary context of the Matthean Lord's Prayer, 6:1–18

> is more about what one should avoid, and about a new pattern of thought . . . to promote an attitude of devotion [and] the very essence of giving alms, prayer and fasting, that is, purification, loving your neighbour and devotion to God . . . [to which] Matt 5.20 . . . is the key: the righteousness that surpasses that of the Pharisees and Scribes.[12]

By connecting almsgiving, prayer and fasting with Matthew's concept of righteousness, Baasland hints at a very important aspect of identity formation in Matthew's Gospel narrative. His connection of the Lord's Prayer with righteousness presents the Prayer's function as a presentation of the content of Jesus's declarations of righteousness, which is a principal requirement for entrance to the Kingdom of God (5:20; 6:33). The Lord's Prayer participates in character formation because it outlines beliefs and practices that provide the basis of this formation within the Matthean community. Du Toit seems to develop similar nuances as Baasland concerning the function of the Matthean Lord's Prayer in identity formation, though in this article he makes no reference to Baasland.

5.2.2 Du Toit

Du Toit suggests that the Lord's Prayer is reflective of the authority of the historical Jesus addressing conflict in the Matthean community. Like Baasland, Du Toit locates the Matthean Lord's Prayer in the triadic literary context of almsgiving (6:2–4), prayer (6:5–15) and fasting (6:16–18). Following Josef Kurzinger and Ulrich Luz, Du Toit similarly regards this position of

---

12. Baasland, *Parables and Rhetoric*, 313–14.

the Lord's Prayer in Matt 6:7–15 either as post-Matthean or Matthean interpolation. Siding with Luz's position regarding Matthean interpolation, Du Toit contends that Matthew inserted 6:7–15 into his version of the Lord's Prayer, because "he regarded it as vital to the Christian understanding of prayer and that to him, as a careful redactor, the insertion made good sense in spite of the disproportionate bulkiness it created" in the narrative.[13] In this case, Du Toit highlights a new perspective on the Lord's Prayer which is lacking in Baasland, namely; that Matthew inserted 6:7–15 to give the prayer a Christian flavor. Not only does the interpolation of 6:7–15 allow the implied author of Matthew's Gospel to use the Lord's Prayer to present the content of a righteousness that he contrasts with the one inculcated by Jewish leadership (6:1–2), but also it encourages the Matthean community to seek honor not from the public but from God.

Moreover, Du Toit regards the Matthean Lord's Prayer as addressing concern for communal freedom. Du Toit thinks that the Matthean Lord's Prayer bears three "we" petitions which mainly provide "the evident back-to-back relationship"[14] between the requests that people should not be led into temptation but be delivered from evil. This, he points out, signifies that, "our entanglement in sin and our existential need to be freed from evil."[15] However, Du Toit did not note the contribution of the pronoun ἡμῶν (pronoun: "our") in stressing the communal perspective of the prayer in 6:9, which also reflects the liturgical setting of the prayer. In this case, the importance of the pronoun ἡμῶν denotes the Matthean community as part of the household of God, because of reference to God as their Father. Finally, Du Toit concludes, "the life situation of Matthew's Syrian, real world receptors influenced his redaction and presentation of the SM (Sermon on the Mount: Matt 5–7) to a noticeable degree," in order to affirm, "the special identity of Jesus's new, end time community."[16] Although Du Toit does not elaborate this conclusion further, his claim here adds weight to the argument that the composition of the Matthean Lord's Prayer as part of Matthew's Gospel was shaped by concerns for reconstructing and legitimating a Christian identity for the community of Matthew as I will explain in due course.

13. Du Toit, "Revisiting the Sermon on the Mount," 86.
14. Du Toit, "Revisiting the Sermon on the Mount," 86.
15. Du Toit, "Revisiting the Sermon on the Mount," 88.
16. Du Toit, "Revisiting the Sermon on the Mount," 87.

5.2.3 Reconstructing a Christian Cultural Identity through Recategorization

At this juncture, it is crucial to remind ourselves of our definition of identity politics. As already stated earlier in chapter 2 for this study identity politics entails *borrowing and accommodation of beliefs, values and norms of an ancient traditional community by a marginal group to reconstruct their identity through recategorization, identification and contestation in order to overcome domination by a majority group and achieve the goal of encouraging non-violent attitude, advocate social good and promote an inclusive household*. Consequently, it is important to think of the function of Matthean Lord's Prayer in terms of reconstructing rather than constructing the identity of the Matthean community. In other words, Matthew felt that the community had an identity that for some reason he felt was inadequate and therefore needed to be changed through a process of reconstruction as elaborated by Matthew's rhetorical use of the concepts of Πάτερ ἡμῶν (Our Father), βασιλεία (Kingdom) and ἄρτος (Bread).

5.2.3.1 Matt 6:9: Πάτερ ἡμῶν.

In his redaction of the Q source, Matthew probably added the personal pronoun ἡμῶν (our) in Matt 6:9 since the original Q probably only had the vocative masculine singular Πάτερ (Father) that is retained in the shorter Lucan Prayer invocation (Luke 11:2). With respect to the redactional activity of Matthew, two issues in the Lord's Prayer stand out. The first issue has to do with the shorter Lukan version. Both Luke and Matthew used the Q source independently, and, therefore, redacted it from Q for their respective audience. Both prayers begin by invoking God as Πάτερ.[17] This Prayer is witnessed by ancient manuscripts such as ℵ, P^{75}, B, 1., 700, pc vol *Syr* showing that it is the earliest form of the phrase. Second, Matthew's longer version of the Prayer witnessed by, W, Z, and f^1 from the point of the text of the Greek New Testament includes a later version of the phrase whereby the prayer begins with a possessive case Πάτερ ἡμῶν (Our Father).[18] Because of the plural form of ἡμῶν in the address of God as Πάτερ, Matthew's version of the Lord's Prayer is characterized as a community prayer that regards God as the metaphorical father of the community, and by implication the

---

17. Rodgers and Rodgers, *Exegetical Key*, 135.
18. See NA28, 195.

members of the community as part of God's family.[19] The literary function of ποιέω (practice) in 6:1 is action, or praxis oriented. Thus, the imperatival προσεύχομαι (pray, prostrate) in 6:9 signals the ritual characteristics of the Matthean Lord's Prayer. Nel noted that in Matthew's version, "rituals function in a complex manner . . . existing rituals . . . serve to reinforce them, while others reinterpret, and even nullify."[20] Thus, the Matthean Lord's Prayer reflects Matthew's appropriation of Jesus's interpretation of earlier Jewish Prayers to provide a cultic perspective. This cultic aspect is important not only in reconstructing the Christian identity of the Matthean community but also maintaining such an identity on account of its regular performance as explained in the following three ways.

Firstly, in its political function, whereby the prayer mimics the *pater-patria* status of the Roman emperors. Porter cites a late first-century BCE calendrical inscription from the Roman province of Asia that honors Augusts in terms of "Father Zeus and savior of the universe." This was a tradition that was applied to honoring the divine status of subsequent Roman emperors, including Nero, who was described in Athens as "good god Asclepius Caesar . . . and Apollo in Athens."[21] Thus, in the Roman Empire, *pater-patria* was an ideology that was probably applied as a political strategy by either the senate or individuals to honor the divine connection of the surviving emperor. It also provided an important aspect of delineating the peoples' identity by symbolically connecting them with the legacy of Caesar Augustus. By imitating the Roman political use of the term *pater-patria*, the Matthean Lord's Prayer assumes a political function that ironically contests and symbolically inverts the political power of the Roman emperor by emphasizing the political power of God as taught by Jesus in the Prayer. The phrase Πάτερ ἡμῶν ὁ ἐν τοῖς οὐρανοῖς (our Father who is in the heavens), in Matt 6:9, is intended to shape the community's self-understanding or sense of identity. This identity-forming role of the prayer is communicated in two ways.

On the one hand, from a ritual perspective, Matthew intends to preserve a twofold communal memory. According to Baker, memory has two phases by which it reconstructs and maintains social identity. The 'communicative' phase is characterized by face-to-face circulation of facts and information, while the cultural memory phase focuses on the past and is

---

19. Osborne, *Matthew*, 227.
20. Nel, "Forgiveness of Debt," 120.
21. Porter, "Paul Confronts Caesar," 170, 173.

comprised of reusable texts, images and rituals.[22] By revising material from the Q source to appropriate Jesus's interpretation of Jewish prayer, Matthew depicts the communicative characteristic of the Lord's Prayer, by which he intends to present its ritual nature to his immediate audience. Moreover, the act of composing the Lord's Prayer indicates that Matthew attempted to preserve the cultural memory of the prayer for future generations of Christians. On the other hand, by redacting Q source through adding the pronoun ἡμῶν in Matt 6:9, Matthew employs the Lord's Prayer to reconstruct a Christian cultural identity of his community by recategorization. This is attained not only through communication and cultural memory, but also through the depersonalizing effect achieved in the recitation of the Prayer by both Judeans and Gentile followers of Jesus. Thus, to reinforce group cohesion, the narrative of the Gospel of Matthew depicts Matthew, the implied author, as a prototypical in-group leader of the community. This depiction to the community ideologically entailed subordinating previous ethnic identity to the superordinate category created and maintained by the memory prompted by oral recitation of the Lord's Prayer.

Second, Neyrey following Malina, comments on the political function of the Lord's Prayer in reference to the Roman patron-client strategy. He says that the phrase Πάτερ ἡμῶν (our father) in Matt 6:9–15

> fully acknowledges the basic patron-client relationship [between the Matthean community] and God. God-patron earthly clients render honor by acclaiming God as heavenly father, whose name is most praiseworthy and whose power and sovereignty should be acknowledged (6:9–10). Once they have paid their dues of honor to the Patron, clients may ask for benefaction, such as food, deliverance from debt, and protection (6:11–13).[23]

Neyrey's comment implies that the narrator of Matthew's Gospel employs the phrase Πάτερ ἡμῶν in the Matthean Lord's Prayer to contest the beneficence of the emperors and elites to render irrelevant the political power of Rome, which was secured through the client-patron strategy in the Matthean community. Thus, regarding God as their father in heaven whose kingdom should come to earth is to replace the role of the Roman emperor and the elites with the invisible God as the father of the Matthean community.

---

22. Baker, *Identity*, 14–16; Baker, "Narrative-Identity Model," 110–12.
23. Neyrey, *Honor and Shame*, 110.

MATTHEW 6:9–13 AND CONSTRUCTION OF IDENTITY POLITICS

Third, in respect to the relations between the Matthean community and Diaspora Judaism, the Matthean Lord's Prayer accomplishes two important tasks. First, Matthew accommodated earlier Judean liturgical traditions. In addition to the invocation of the original, the Q prayer resonates with the Judean אָבִינוּ (our Father) in the Kaddish and Shimoneh Esreh types of Jewish prayers. These were likely significant in the formation of Jewish identity among the Judeans in the Diaspora, as highlighted in chapter four. Consequently, not only did Matthew edit what he found in the Q tradition, but he accommodated Jewish traditions of prayer so as to provide a belief system for his community when constructing a cultural identity as a family of God in similar terms as first-century Judeans sectarian communities understood their identity. As mentioned, either the Matthean community was a Judean sectarian group regarding itself as part of true Israel or, unfortunately, a deviant Judean group struggling with other Judean sectarian groups in contextualizing traditional Judean religious sources to constitute a new community in the post-70 CE period, or even worse still, a deviant Judean group within formative Judaism that sought to legitimate its religious identity. It is also more unfortunately commonly claimed that it was a deviant Judean community seeking to establish a new symbolic universe without denying the way it was previously understood,[24] or as one form of middle Judaism with a distinct synagogue-derived identity.[25] Underlying all these assumptions is a conception of the Matthean community relations with Diaspora Judaism.

In view of the above scenarios, there are three reasons which suggest that during the composition of the Gospel of Matthew, the Matthean community was in the process of separating from Diaspora Judaism to strengthen their belonging to the Jesus Movement. At the time, full separation of the Matthean community with first-century Diaspora Judaism had not yet taken place. (1) Matthew regarded the crowd as potential members of the Matthean community because he was sympathetic to them while at the same time vilifying the Judean leadership (Matt 5:1; 7:23); (2) Matthew's narrative shows commonality and affinity between Matthew's community with other members of the Jesus Movement regarding baptism as the entrance rite (3:10; Luke 3:9; Mark 1:8; Acts 1:5; 2:37–38; Rom 6:4) as well as a complementary position regarding Paul's position on works

---

24. Riches, "Social World of Jesus," 61, 64; Saldarini, *Matthew's Christian-Jewish Community*, 66–68.

25. Talbert, *Sermon on the Mount*, 6.

of Law (Matt 5:17; Gal 2:6); and (3) Matthew's text (10:17) creates the impression (not necessarily a historical event) of the flogging of members of the Jesus Movement by Jewish synagogue leadership. Given these three reasons, the best position would be to regard the Matthean community as experiencing a liminal Judean identity. That is; an identity that is at the intersection of Judean cultural identity and a pro-Jesus Movement identity. At the time of the composition of the Gospel of Matthew, the Matthean community was gradually losing grip of their Judean ethnic identity, while at the same time getting acquainted with a sub-cultural Christian identity that they are learning to accept. In other words, the relationship between the Matthean community and Diaspora Judaism is like that of independent siblings, who, although they have the same parents, nonetheless they are gradually acquiring their own independent homesteads for their families. This resonates with McIver's position that the Matthean community continued to show a positive attitude to the Law, circumcision, dietary purity, Sabbath observance, etc. McIver claims that by maintaining a positive attitude to Judean cultural beliefs and values, the Matthean community was part of mainstream Christianity, not some marginal community living in the past.[26] How does Matthew's Lord's Prayer participate in legitimating the Judeo-Christian identity of the Matthean community? In what follows, I attempt to answer this question.

5.2.4 Legitimating a Christian Identity through Identification

Matt 6:10 depicts the reconstruction and legitimation of the Christian identity of the Matthean community in relation to Judean and Roman understandings of Kingdom, to communicate to the Matthean community why Rome and all earthly power possessed by elites should not be regarded as important for the Matthean community where God's Kingdom and God's will would prevail.

5.2.4.1 Matt 6.10: βασιλεία

The question of the function of βασιλεία (Kingdom), in Matt 6:10, has been a matter of debate among New Testament scholars. Osborne views the second petition, Ἐλθέτω ἡ βασιλεία σου (let you Kingdom come), in

---

26. McIver, *Mainstream or Marginal?*, 160–61.

Matt 6:10, as an eschatological element of the Lord's Prayer that requests "God [to] end this present order and bring the Kingdom in fullness."[27] Osborne is right in so far as he regards the prayer as establishing the sovereignty of God on earth through Jesus's sayings. This is in line with Christian interpretation of the Isaian prophetic narratives, according to which Isaiah prophesied the birth of Jesus as a royal child, saying, "For to us a child is borne, to us a son is given, and the government will be on his shoulders. And he will be called wonderful Counsellor, Mighty God, Everlasting Father, Prince of Peace" (Isa 9:5–6). However, Osborne fails to notice how Matthew borrows from Jewish traditions to mimic Roman imperial political influence. Josephus (*BJ* 2.390) noted the confession of King Agrippa II (c. 27–100 CE), saying to his fellow Judeans, "What remains, therefore, is this, that you have recourse to Divine assistance; but this is already on the side of the Romans; for it is impossible that so vast an empire should be settled without God's providence." Coupled with the understanding that Jupiter sanctioned the founding of Rome, Agrippa's words confirm the mythical belief surviving in the late first-century CE of the divine status of the Roman Empire. So, while inter textually Isaiah (9:5–6) testifies to Matthew's borrowing from Hebrew traditions, even though it is never quoted, such borrowing was intended to emphasize the political function of the Lord's Prayer by contesting popular belief in the divine origin of the Roman empire. Carter aptly claims that Matthew 6:10 "underlines the importance and longing for God to recreate the world" by changing the devil's claims symbolized by the Roman Empire.[28]

Matthew 6:10 indicates Matthew's borrowing from Hebrew and Judean traditions regarding God as King to boost the political function of the Lord's Prayer, to identify his community with these traditions, and to outline beliefs for his community concerning God's Kingdom. In Hebrew traditions—for instance in Isaiah 6:5—God's Kingdom signifies his reign or authority, which, in the light of Rabbinic Mishnah traditions (*Sifra A. M pq* 13:194.2.1; *Sifre Deut* 313:1.3; 323:1.2), signifies God's present rule. God's future rule, where he will rule unchallenged, is outlined in Isaiah 9:6–7; 24:23; 52:7; *Sifra Behuq. pq.* 8:269.2.3.[29] This present and future rule of God is attested in the Kaddish Yatom and Shimoneh Esreh, briefly explored in the previous sections. Viewed in the context of heaven (Matt 6:9) to imply "Kingdom of

---

27. Osborne, *Matthew*, 228.
28. Carter, *Matthew and the Margins*, 165.
29. Keener, *Gospel of Matthew*, 68.

heaven," the Matthean Lord's Prayer further contests citizenship granted by Roman political authority, to boost peoples' honor as supported by Keener, citing Rom 8:23, Eph 1:13–14, and Heb 6:4–5, saying that

> The present significance of the future kingdom in early Christian teaching was thus that God's people in the present age were citizens of the coming age, people whose identity was determined by what Jesus had done and what they would be, not by what they had been or by their status in the world.[30]

In this case, identification with Hebrew and Judean tradition provided a basis for setting out a belief system for the Matthean community in reference to God's Kingdom. This belief system created a basis for legitimating cultural status of the identity for Matthew's community. Not only did Matthew apply his version of the Lord's Prayer to emphasize the political aspect of the prayer, but he also intended to stress the economic aspect of it, as will be discussed from the point of view of Matt 6:11 in the following section.

5.2.4.2 Matt 6:11: ἄρτος

Davies and Allison regard 6:11 as reflective of Jesus's teaching rather than a reference to the manna from heaven (Exod 16). The eschatological beliefs of some Judeans (2 Bar 29.8) and the Jesus Movement (Matt 8:11; Luke 22:28–30) suggest an "anticipation of the eschatological banquet."[31] Davies and Allison's refusal to see a connection between manna and ἄρτος (bread) is refuted in the discussion that follows. Davies and Allison note that 6:11 is reflective of Judean eschatological expectation because "the material bread which God gives today transparently symbolizes and foreshadows the eschatological bread [manna], which will bring lasting satisfaction."[32] While Davies and Allison aptly observe the eschatological function of ἄρτος they fail to see the economic function of this prayer. Coupled with ἀφίημι (forgive), in 6:12, Nel says Matthew's Lord's Prayer refers to "demands for remission of every exploitative [economic] debt."[33] In the context of the beneficence role of the Roman emperor and Roman elites, Matthew's Lord's Prayer had an economic function in his community for the Jesus-believers;

---

30. Keener, *Gospel of Matthew*, 69.
31. Davies and Allison, *Saint Matthew*, 609.
32. Davies and Allison, *Saint Matthew*, 609.
33. Nel, "Forgiveness of Debt," 102.

God is a more reliable patron or more beneficent than the emperor or the Roman elite. As noted by Luke (13:14; Acts 18:18), ἀρχισυνάγωγος refers to a synagogue ruler, a category of Roman elite. In the Roman Empire, not only were the elites charged with political authority, but they also had to dispense beneficence, just like the emperor, in order to meet the economic needs of the local communities. In their article, "*Archisynagogoi*: Office, Title and Social Status in the Greco-Jewish Synagogue," Tessa Rajak and David Noy observe the role of the non-Judean status requirements for Synagogue rulers to accomplish their elite role in the diaspora. They argue:

> The archisynagogos was a patronal figure. With his wealth, his high standing, and the advantage of a title which the outside world could recognize instantly, he had the wherewithal to act as a mediator for community. It is conceivable, indeed that you did not have to be a Jewish to be an Archisynagogos. It may have been enough to take patronal interest in a Jewish community.[34]

Rajak and Noy indicate how in the post 66–73 CE Jewish war, Roman elites in pursuit of their mediatorial role usurped the authority of the Sanhedrin in providing social, economic and political leadership to the Judeans in the Diaspora. This observation is reflective of the replacement of the traditional qualifications for synagogue rulers. In other words, for one to qualify as a ruler of a synagogue, they were required "to exercise beneficence and patronage in the Roman society," as noted by Carter.[35] The qualification was not necessarily Judean ethnicity, but one's "elite social standing."

Matthew employs a two-way approach to contest the beneficence found in the Roman Empire supported by imperial rule. On the one hand and contrary to Davies and Allison, he accommodated from Hebrew tradition the miraculous provisions of manna (Exod 16). On the other hand, he borrowed traditions of the Jesus Movement such as Mark 6:37–42; Luke 9:13–17; 11:1–4, to contest the beneficence strategy of the Roman Empire in order to emphasize the economic function of his Lord's Prayer. Through this accommodation and borrowing, Matthew accomplished two important economic goals that were significant in legitimating the Judeo-Christian identity of his community. One, the accommodating of Judean and Jesus traditions was intended to mark the continuity of Judean beliefs regarding the providence of God, which was carried over from the Jesus Movement. This belief was important for legitimating both a Judean

---

34. Rajak and Noy, "*Archisynagogoi*," 88.
35. Carter, "Matthew," 289.

and a Christian identity in the Matthean community. Two, by emphasizing the request for God's daily provision of bread, the Matthean Lord's Prayer subordinates the economic aspect of the Roman imperial use of beneficence to God's economic provisions as petitioned in the Lord's Prayer. Matt 6:25–33 helps in elaborating the significance of 6:11 because "do not worry" in Matt 6:25 is an attempt to forbid anxiety which is ordinarily provoked by socio-economic and political injustice.[36] In order to urge trust in God, this passage (6:25–33) attempts to contest some injustices arising from the Roman Empire. Literarily, the connection of petition for ἄρτος in 6:11 to righteousness is facilitated by 6:25–33 to emphasize God's care for his people in opposition to Roman beneficence. This connects striving for the Kingdom of God with God's righteousness that leads to God giving the necessities of life to the followers of Jesus.

5.3 A Social-Evangelistic Identity Politics

This is the question we want to address here: how does Dawn Moon's social evangelism mode facilitate the goal of identity politics envisioned in this study, namely, encouraging a non-violent attitude, advocating social good and promoting an inclusive household? Matthew's version of the Lord's Prayer in 6:9–13 delineates the prospects of identity politics for the community of Matthew. The group relations emerging from the exploration of Matthew's Lord's Prayer provide some insights for Matthew's social evangelistic identity politics. There are three functions of social evangelistic identity politics which in effect are instrumental in accomplishing the goal of identity politics. These are; accommodation of the Jewish traditions, identification with Israel traditions and appropriating Jesus's prayers. These functions, correspondingly, encourage a non-violent attitude, advocate for social good and, promote an inclusive household.

5.3.1 Accommodating Jewish Tradition to Encourage Non-violent Attitude

Through accommodating Jewish traditions to contest Roman political power (6:9–10), the narrator hopes to accomplish some aspects of social

---

36. Barton, *Discipleship and Family Ties*, 140–55; Carter, *Matthew and the Margins*, 176; Kingsbury, "On Following Jesus," 45–59.

evangelism related to the transformation of individuals. Given the violent response to Roman oppression in the first Jewish revolt, which led to the destruction of the second Jerusalem temple, the hearers of the Gospel of Matthew were persuaded to focus on God's intervention by praying for the Kingdom of God to come (6:10). The discourse of the Matthean Lord's Prayer was attempting to initiate a process of transformation of the violent attitudes of some Judeans towards Roman rule. According to Josephus (*BJ* 2:342–44) during the beginning of the war in 66 CE, some Jews resisted violence, and instead preferred to use a diplomatic approach to resolve their grievances with Rome. The goal of this process was to adopt a non-violent, pacifist attitude towards matters of conflict. Similarly, proponents of social evangelism hope to achieve the transformation based on a "fluid conception of the self"[37] which emphasizes the possibility of shifting personal inclination towards violence to a non-violent stance on account of one's personal decision. Thus, by employing the concept of βασιλεία (Kingdom) to focus people's attention on the sovereignty of God, the Matthean Lord's Prayer aimed at recruiting a community from both ethnic Judeans and Gentiles that would see themselves as having been transformed from unredeemed to redeemed selves by joining the Matthean community. The role of Matthew's concept of βασιλεία, in accomplishing this transformation agenda of social movement evangelism is further rationalized by the narrative's focus on "the lost sheep of Israel" (Matt 10:6) and missions to the surrounding nations (Matt 28:18–20).

5.3.2 Identification with Israel to Advocate for Social Good

Given the legitimation of the Judeo-Christian identity of the Matthean community, Overman's claim that the Matthean community regarded itself as "the true Israel" becomes plausible.[38] Identification with Israel ideologically empowered the Matthean community to employ social movement evangelism. The social evangelism mode of identity politics, according to Moon, is premised on the argument that in the society there are two options, either of the good or bad (proponents of social evangelism identity politics see themselves standing on the good side). Members conceive themselves as having the social responsibility of helping people to choose to reject the bad side in order to follow the good side. By regarding themselves as "the true Israel," the

---

37. Moone, "Who Am I?," 1369.
38. Overman, *Matthew's Gospel*, 5.

Matthean community sought to reclaim Israel's covenant privileges. Given the status of "true Israel", by which the Matthean community "set themselves over against those they believed to be false covenant people and false leaders who lead the people astray," the community attempted to accomplish social evangelism by perceiving the failed Judean leadership as fundamentally evil, while at the same time understanding themselves as righteous, and therefore, regarding themselves as God's true people.[39]

5.3.3 Appropriating Jesus's Prayers to Promote an Inclusive Household

Matthew's addition of ἡμῶν (possessive pronoun: "our") to his Lord's Prayer (6:9) shows his intention to appropriate prayers interpreted by Jesus to his disciples, in order to advance some aspects of his social movement evangelism mode of identity politics in creating a superordinate identity. Because ἡμῶν gives Matthew the advantage of creating an inclusive community, it reveals Matthew's attempts to transform Judean perceptions of a household of God. Since Matthew's social evangelism focused on recruiting the ὄχλους (crowd: 5:1; 8:18; 9:36; 13:36; 21:46), τὰ πρόβατα τὰ ἀπολωλότα οἴκου Ἰσραήλ (the lost sheep of the house of Israel; 10:6) and τὰ ἔθνη (non-Judean, Gentiles, pagan; 12:21; 25:32; 28:19), he most likely decided to include ἡμῶν in his Lord's Prayer to emphasize the inclusive rather than the exclusive perspective of his community as God's household. This perspective, in stressing the inclusive aspect of the Lord's Prayer, transforms not only the perception, but also the practice of the exclusive lifestyle of households in Diaspora Judaism.

Thus the narrator's application of the Lord's Prayer to meet concerns of social evangelistic identity politics refutes Overman's notion that during its emergence, the Matthean community was "concerned with world maintenance" and was interested in "community formation," but "not primarily world transformation."[40] The social evangelism mode of identity politics on its own gives a sort of monolithic interpretation of the Lord's Prayer. Consequently, the multivalent aspect of the Lord's Prayer and its function in securing a social evangelistic mode of identity politics presents the Lord's Prayer not only as contesting and accommodating socio-economic and political norms and values in the Roman Empire, but this contestation and

---

39. Overman, *Matthew's Gospel*, 5.
40. Overman, *Matthew's Gospel*, 154.

accommodation entailed a transformation of these norms and values. This demonstrates the interest of Matthew to employ his version of the Lord's Prayer to transform late first century Greco-Jewish world.

5.4 Conclusion

The function of the pronoun ἡμῶν and the concepts βασιλεία of God and ἄρτος in the Matthean Lord's Prayer demonstrate the ideological significance of Matthew's concept of righteousness in Matt 5:20 as elaborated in 6:25–33. By employing these three concepts, Matthew's narrative attempted to construct a superordinate identity category for the Matthean community that facilitated what the Jewish prayers, particularly, the Kaddish, and Shimoneh Esreh, could not accomplish. Ideologically, the Kaddish and Shimoneh Esreh prayers facilitated a limited vision of God's household, one which was limited to Judeans and in which Gentiles were regarded as outsiders and unrighteous people. The function of Matthew's Lord's Prayer was to affect a social evangelistic identity politics that focused on accommodating non-violent attitude, advocating social good and promoting an inclusive household. By focusing on both Judeans and Gentiles, Matthew's Lord's Prayer demonstrates the ideological function of Matthew's concept of righteousness in 5:20. In reference to the Matthean Lord's Prayer, the efficacy of Jesus's prayer was intended to affect the aspirations of a social evangelistic identity politics that focused on an inclusive household of God. This in turn provided socio-economic and political power to negotiate the cultural identity of the community in the Roman Empire. The socio-economic and political aspects of the Matthean Lord's Prayer ideologically exuded the potency of a righteousness which surpasses that of the teachers of the law and Pharisees, pagans, and hypocrites in the Antiochene society.

CHAPTER 6

CONCLUSION

To address the question of how Matthew's uses his version of the Lord's Prayer to elaborate the rhetorical function of his concept of righteousness in shaping the identity of his community in the late first century CE, it is crucial to describe the dynamics of the SRAT to present textual interpretative principles, to apply aspects of inter textual analysis to read the literary function of Matthew's version of the Lord's Prayer, to explore identity formation in Roman Empire, the Jesus's Movement and Diaspora Judaism to provide the social setting of the community of Matthew.

The rhetorical functions of selected concepts such as the pronoun ἡμῶν (our) and the nouns βασιλεία (Kingdom) and ἄρτος (bread) in the Matthean Lord's Prayer has been undertaken to demonstrate the ideological significance of Matthew's concept of righteousness. By employing these three concepts, Matthew's narrative attempted to construct a superordinate identity category for the Matthean community that facilitated what the Jewish prayers, particularly, the Kaddish, and Shimoneh Esreh, could not accomplish. Ideologically, the Kaddish and Shimoneh Esreh prayers facilitated a limited vision of God's household, one which was limited to Judeans and in which Gentiles were regarded as outsiders and unrighteous people. The function of Matthew's Lord's Prayer was to affect a social evangelistic identity politics that focused on accommodating non-violent attitude, advocating social good and promoting an inclusive household. By focusing on both Judeans and Gentiles, Matthew's Lord's Prayer demonstrates the ideological function of Matthew's concept of righteousness in 5:20. In reference to the Matthean Lord's Prayer, the efficacy of Jesus's prayer was intended to affect the aspirations of a social evangelistic identity politics that focused on an inclusive household of God. This in turn provided socio-economic and political power to negotiate the cultural identity of the Matthean community in the Roman Empire. The socio-economic and political aspects of the

CONCLUSION

Matthean Lord's Prayer ideologically exuded the potency of a righteousness which surpasses that of the teachers of the law and Pharisees, pagans, and hypocrites in the Antiochene society.

In other words, the focus of this book, *The Lord's Prayer in Matthew 6:9–13* has been to use socio-rhetorical analysis theory to describe Matthew's perspective of identity politics in reference to a triad trajectory of relationship between the community of Mathew with the Roman Empire, Diaspora Judaism and the Jesus Movement in the late first century CE Syrian Antioch. A brief review of New Testament scholarship has shown although traditional use of literary analysis of the Lord's Prayer portrays the potency for describing the theological significance of the Prayer, it falls short of inferring the group relations of Matthew's community with their neighbors, an aspect of Biblical study achieved through socio-rhetorical analysis, a qualitative research method that blends literary and social scientific models. This approach has been applied in this book to answer the question: what was the significance of the Matthew's Lord's Prayer to his community in the late first-century CE? Consequently, the argument that Matthew employs his version of the Lord's Prayer to recategorize his community into a superordinate identity through identification with Jewish religious traditions, through contesting Roman political and economic claims of benefices, and through accommodating the liturgical traditions of the Jesus Movement, has been defended in this book. The findings of this book not only demonstrated the contribution of interdisciplinary research method, that is, an approach that blends literary criticism with sociological and anthropological concepts, in religious studies, but also reveals the value of observing first century CE social setting for elaborating the discourse of early Christian communities. The conclusion arrived at in this study is that taking note of the trajectories of relationships of any given community to subject these group relations to a socio-rhetorical analysis has the potency to reveal the underlying aspects of identity politics of the community embedded in a given text whether a literary or artifact or archeological text. The values, norms and traditions emerging from such a rhetorical function of texts essentially inform the community's identity.

BIBLIOGRAPHY

Adams, Geoff W. "Suetonius and His Treatment of the Emperor Domitian's Favourable Accomplishments." *Studia Humaniora Tartuensia* 6.A.3 (2005) 1–15.

Adeyemo, Tokunboh, ed. *Africa Bible Commentary*. Nairobi: Word Alive, 2006.

Ando, Clifford. *A Matter of the Gods: Religion and Empire*. Berkeley: University of California Press, 2008.

"Arch of Titus, Rome." https://www.romecitytour.it/attractions/arch-of-titus/.

Baasland, Ernst. *Parables and Rhetoric in the Sermon on the Mount*. WUNT 351. Tubingen: Mohr Siebeck, 2015.

Baker, Coleman A. *Identity, Memory, and Narrative in Early Christianity*. Eugene, OR: Pickwick, 2011.

———. "A Narrative-Identity Model for Biblical Interpretation: The Role of Memory and Narrative in Social Identity Formation." In *T&T Clark Handbook to Social Identity in the New Testament*, edited by J. Brian Tucker and Coleman A. Baker, 105–18. London: Bloomsbury, 2016.

Barclay, John M. G. *Jews in the Mediterranean Diaspora: From Alexander to Trajan from 323 BCE to 117 CE*. Edinburgh: T. & T. Clark, 1999.

Barr, D. L. "The Lamb Who Looks Like a Dragon? Characterizing Jesus in John's Apocalypse." In *The Reality of Apocalypse: Rhetoric and Politics in the Book of Revelation*, edited by David L. Barr, 205–20. Symposium Series 39. Atlanta: Society of Biblical Literature, 2006.

Barton, Stephen C. *Discipleship and Family Ties in Mark and Matthew*. Society for New Testament Studies Monograph Series 80. Cambridge: Cambridge University Press, 1994.

Bauer, Walter, et al. *A Greek-English Lexicon of the New Testament and Early Christian Literature*. Chicago: University of Chicago Press, 2000.

Berger, Peter L. *The Sacred Canopy: Elements of Sociological Theory*. Garden City, NY: Doubleday, 1969.

Bernstein, Mary. "Identity Politics." *Annual Review of Sociology* 31 (2005) 47–74.

Betz, Hans Dieter. *The Sermon on the Mount: A Commentary on the Sermon on the Mount, Including the Sermon on the Plain (Matthew 5:3–7:27 and Luke 6:20–49)*. Hermeneia. Minneapolis: Fortress, 1995.

Book 2 of Baruch. https://irp-cdn.multiscreensite.com/15d2699b/files/uploaded/book-2-of-Baruch%20.pdf.

Carter, Warren. *Matthew and the Margins: A Socio-Political and Religious Reading*. Bible & Liberation Series. Maryknoll, NY: Orbis, 2000.

———. "Matthew: Empire, Synagogues, and Horizontal Violence." In *Mark and Matthew 1: Comparative Readings: Understanding the Earliest Gospels in Their First Century Settings*, edited by Eve-Marrie Becker and Anderson Runneson, 285–308. WUNT 271. Tubingen: Mohr Siebeck, 2011.

Case, Shirley Jackson. "Origin and Purpose of the Gospel of Matthew." *The Biblical World* 34.6 (1909) 390–402.

Charles, R. H., trans. "The Assumption of Moses." In vol. 2 of *The Apocrypha and Pseudepigrapha of the Old Testament in English*, 407–24. Oxford: Clarendon, 1913. http://wesley.nnu.edu/index.php?id=2124.

Chua, Amy. *Day of Empire: How Hyperpowers Rise to Global Dominance and Why They Fall*. New York: Doubleday, 2007.

Cirafesi, Wally V. "The Johannine Community Hypothesis (1968–Present): Past and Present Approaches and a New Way Forward." *Currents in Biblical Research* 12 (2014) 173–93.

Cohen, Shaye J. D. "The Ways That Parted: Jews, Christians, and Jewish-Christian ca. 100–150 CE." *Near Eastern Languages and Civilizations* (2013) 1–34.

Columella. *On Agriculture, Volume I: Books 1–4*. Translated by Harrison Boyd Ash. Loeb Classical Library 361. Cambridge: Harvard University Press, 1941.

Crossan, John Dominic. *The Birth of Christianity: Discovering What Really Happened in the Years Immediately after the Execution of Jesus*. San Francisco: HarperSanFrancisco, 1998.

Davies, W. D., and Dale C. Allison. *A Critical and Exegetical Commentary on the Gospel according to Saint Matthew*. Vol. 1, *Introduction and Commentary on Matthew I–VII*. International Critical Commentary. Edinburgh: T. & T. Clark, 1988.

Dio Cassius. *Roman History, Volume VIII: Books 61–70*. Translated by Earnest Cary and Herbert B. Foster. Loeb Classical Library 176. Cambridge: Harvard University Press, 1925.

Drake, Lyndon. "Did Jesus Oppose the *Prosbul* in the Forgiveness Petition of the Lord's Prayer?" *NovTest* 56 (2014) 233–44.

Du Toit, Andrie B. "Revisiting the Sermon on the Mount: Some Major Issues." *Neot* 50.3 (2016) 59–91.

Duling, Dennis C. "Empire: Theories, Methods, Models." In *The Gospel of Matthew in Its Roman Imperial Context*, edited by John K. Riches and David C. Sim, 49–74. London: T. & T. Clark, 2005.

Dunn, J. D. G. *Jews and Christians: The Parting of the Ways, AD 70 to 135*. Grand Rapids: Eerdmans, 1992.

———. "Pharisees, Sinners, and Jesus." In *The Social World of the Formative Christianity and Judaism*, edited by Jacob Neusner et al., 246–89. Philadelphia: Fortress, 1988.

Eagleton, Terry. *Literary Theory: An Introduction*. Minneapolis: University of Minnesota Press, 1983.

Esler, Philip Francis. *Conflict and Identity in Romans: The Social Setting of Paul's Letter*. Minneapolis: Ausburg Fortress, 2003.

———. *The First Christians in Their Social Worlds: Social-Scientific Approaches to New Testament Interpretation*. London: Routledge, 1994.

———. "Group Norms and Prototypes in Matthew 5.3–12: A Social Identity Interpretation of the Matthean Beatitudes." In *T&T Clark Handbook to Social Identity in the New Testament*, edited by J. Brian Tucker and Coleman A. Baker, 147–71. London: Bloomsbury, 2016.

BIBLIOGRAPHY

———. "Rome in Apocalyptic and Rabbinic Literature." In *The Gospel of Matthew in Its Roman Imperial Context*, edited by John K. Riches and David C. Sim, 9–33. London: T. & T. Clark, 2005.

Eusebius. "Church History." In Vol. 1 of *Nicene and Post-Nicene Fathers, Second Series*, edited by Philip Schaff and Henry Wace, translated by Arthur Cushman McGiffert. Revised and edited for *New Advent* by Kevin Knight. Buffalo, NY: Christian Literature, 1890. http://www.newadvent.org/fathers/2501.htm.

Evans, Craig A., and H. Daniel Zacharias. *What Does the Scripture Say? Studies in the Functions of the Scripture in Early Judaism and Christianity*. London: T. & T. Clark, 2012.

Faulkner, Anne. "Jewish Identity and Jerusalem Conference: Social Identity and Self-Categorization in the Early Church Communities." *E-Sharp* 6.1 (2005) 1–17.

Fogg, Julia Lambert. "Antioch." https://www.bibleodyssey.org/en/tools/Map-gallery/a/map-antioch.

Gager, John G. *Kingdom and Community: The Social World of the Early Christianity*. Englewood Cliffs, NJ: Prentice-Hall, 1975.

Green, Joel B. *1 Peter*. Two Horizons New Testament Commentary. Grand Rapids: Eerdmans, 2007.

Grelot, Pierre. "La Quatrième Demande du 'Pater' et son Arrière-Plan Sèmitique." *NTS* 25.3 (1979) 299–31.

Grivich, Matthew. "The Letters of Paul." http://www.systematicchristianity.org/TheLettersOfPaul.htm.

Guelich, Robert A. *The Sermon on the Mount: A Foundation for Understanding*. Waco, TX: Word, 1982.

———. "The Undivided Way." *Journal of Ecumenical Studies* 14.2 (1977) 233–48.

Hann, Robert R. "The Undivided Way." *Journal of Ecumenical Studies* 14.2 (1977) 233–48.

Hartland, Philip A. *Associations, Synagogues, and Congregations: Claiming Place in Ancient Mediterranean Society*. Minneapolis: Fortress, 2003.

———. "Jesus-in-Movement and the Roman Imperial (Dis)order." In *An Introduction to Empire in the New Testament*, edited by Adam Win, 47–69. Resources for Biblical Study 84. Atlanta: Society of Biblical Literature, 2016.

———. *Paul and Empire: Religion and Power in Roman Imperial Society*. Harrisburg, PA: Trinity, 1997.

———. *Paul and Politics: Ekklesia, Israel, Imperium, Interpretation*. Harrisburg, PA: Trinity, 2000.

Homer. *The Iliad of Homer*. Vol. 1. Translated by Lord Derby. London: Murray, 1865. https://archive.org/details/iliadhomero1derbgoog.

———. *The Odyssey*. Rendered into English prose by Samuel Butler. Revised by Timothy Power and Gregory Nagy. London: Fifield, 1900. http://www.perseus.tufts.edu/hopper/text?doc=Perseus:text:1999.01.0218.

Horsley, Richard A. "Jesus-in-Movement and the Roman Imperial (Dis)order." In *An Introduction to Empire in the New Testament*, edited by Adam Win, 47–69. Atlanta, GA: Society of Biblical Literature, 2016.

———. *Paul and Empire: Religion and Power in Roman Imperial Society*. Harrisburg, PA: Trinity, 1997.

———. *Paul and Politics: Ekklesia, Israel, Imperium, Interpretation*. Harrisburg, PA: Trinity, 1997.

BIBLIOGRAPHY

Huskinson, Janet. "Élite Culture and the Identity of Empire." In *Experiencing Rome: Culture, Identity, and Power in the Roman Empire*, edited by Janet Huskinson, 95–124. London: Routledge, 2009.

———, ed. *Experiencing Rome: Culture, Identity, and Power in the Roman Empire*. London: Routledge, 2009.

———. "Looking for Culture, Identity, and Power." In *Experiencing Rome: Culture, Identity, and Power in the Roman Empire*, edited by Janet Huskinson, 3–28. London: Routledge, 2009.

Ignatius. "The Epistle of Ignatius to the Magnesians." In vol. 1 of *Ante-Nicene Fathers*, edited by Alexander Roberts et al., translated by Alexander Roberts and James Donaldson. Buffalo, NY: Christian Literature, 1885. Revised and edited for *New Advent* by Kevin Knight. http://www.newadvent.org/fathers/0105.htm.

———. "The Epistle of Ignatius to the Philadelphians." In vol. 1 of *Ante-Nicene Fathers*, edited by Alexander Roberts et al., translated by Alexander Roberts and James Donaldson. Buffalo, NY: Christian Literature, 1885. Revised and edited for *New Advent* by Kevin Knight. www.newadvent.org/fathers/0108.htm.

———. "The Epistle of Ignatius to the Smyrnaeans." In vol. 1 of *Ante-Nicene Fathers*, edited by Alexander Roberts et al., translated by Alexander Roberts and James Donaldson. Buffalo, NY: Christian Literature, 1885. Revised and edited for *New Advent* by Kevin Knight. https://www.newadvent.org/fathers/0109.htm.

———. "The Epistle of Ignatius to the Trallians." In vol. 1 of *Ante-Nicene Fathers*, edited by Alexander Roberts et al., translated by Alexander Roberts and James Donaldson. Buffalo, NY: Christian Literature, 1885. Revised and edited for *New Advent* by Kevin Knight. https://www.newadvent.org/fathers/0106.htm.

Jeremias, Joachim. *The Prayers of Jesus*. London: SCM, 1967.

"Jewish Prayers: Mourners Kaddish." https://www.jewishvirtuallibrary.org/the-mourners-kaddish.

Jones, B. W., ed. *Suetonius: Domitian*. London: Bristol Classical, 1996.

Josephus. *Against Apion*. Translated by William Whiston. https://lexundria.com/j_ap/0/wst.

———. *Antiquities of the Jews*. Translated by William Whiston. https://www.lexundria.com/j_aj/0/wst.

———. *Josephus, Complete Works*. Translated by William Whiston. Grand Rapids: Kregel, 1978.

———. *Wars of the Jews*. Translated by William Whiston. https://www.lexundria.com/j_bj/0/wst.

Keener, Craig S. *The Gospel of Matthew: A Socio-Rhetorical Commentary*. Grand Rapids: Eerdmans, 2009.

Kempny, Mirian. "The Cultural Context of Social Knowledge and the Theoretical Foundations of Sociology and Anthropology." *Polish Sociological Bulletin* 93 (1991) 5–16.

Kingsbury, Jack Dean. "On Following Jesus: The Eager Scribe and the Reluctant Disciple (Matthew 8:18–22)." *NTS* 34 (1988) 45–59.

Kittel, Gerhard, and Gerhard Friedrich, eds. *Theological Dictionary of the New Testament*. Translated by Geoffrey W. Bromiley. Grand Rapids: Eerdmans, 1964–76.

Kuecker, Aaron. "Ethnicity and Social Identity." In *T&T Clark Handbook to Social Identity in the New Testament*, edited by J. Brian Tucker and Coleman A. Baker, 59–77. London: Bloomsbury, 2016.

BIBLIOGRAPHY

Lamprecht, Liana. "Reading Matthew 6:13a ('Lead Us Not into Temptation') within the Massâh-Matrix: Biblical and Historical Literary Evidence for a Further Consideration of the Sixth Petition in the Lord's Prayer." *Journal of Early Christian History* 6.3 (2016) 22–42.

M'bwangi, F. Manjewa. "Paul and Identity Construction in Early Christianity and the Roman Empire." *HTS Teologiese Studies/Theological Studies* 76.4 (2020) a5652.

———. "A Reading of the Leper's Healing through Ethnomedical Anthropology." *HTS Teologiese Studies/Theological Studies* 77.1 (2021) a6803.

Mack, Burton L., and Vernon K. Robbins. *Patterns of Persuasion in the Gospels*. Sonoma, CA: Polebridge, 1989.

Malina, Bruce J., and Jerome H. Neyrey. *Portraits of Paul: An Archaeology of Ancient Personality*. Louisville: Westminster John Knox, 1996.

Mann, Michael. *The Source of Social Power*. New York: Cambridge University Press, 2012.

Martyn, J. Louis. *History & Theology in the Fourth Gospel*. 2nd rev. ed. Nashville: Abingdon, 1979.

Mason, Eric F., and Troy W. Martin. *Reading 1–2 Peter and Jude: A Resource for Students*. Atlanta: Society of Biblical Literature, 2014.

May, Herbert G. ed. *Oxford Bible Atlas*. London: Oxford University Press, 1962.

McDonald, Lee Martin. "Antioch (Syria)." In *The Dictionary of New Testament Background*, edited by Craig A. Evans and Stanley Porter, 34–37. Leicester: InterVarsity, 2000.

McIver, Robert K. *Mainstream or Marginal? The Matthean Community in Early Christianity*. Frankfurt: Lang, 2012.

McKnight, Scot. *A Light among the Gentiles: Jewish Missionary Activity in the Second Temple Period*. Minneapolis: Fortress, 1991.

Meeks, Wayne A. "Breaking Away." In *"To See Ourselves" as Others See Us": Christians, Jews, and "Others" in Late Antiquity*, edited Jacob Neusner and Ernest S. Frerichs, 94115. Chico, CA: Scholars, 1985.

———. "The Man from Heaven in Johannine Sectarianism." *Journal of Biblical Literature* 91.1 (1972) 44–72.

Moon, Dawne. "Who Am I and Who Are We? Conflicting Narratives of Collective Selfhood in Stigmatized Groups." *American Journal of Sociology* 117.5 (2012) 1336–79.

Nel, Marius J. "The Forgiveness of Debt in Matthew 6:12, 14–15." *Neot* 47.1 (2013) 87–106.

Neusner, Jacob. "The Formation of Rabbinic Literature: Yavneh (Jamnia) from A.D. 70 to 100." *Aufstieg und Niedergang der römischen Welt* 2.19.2 (1979) 3–42.

———. *Introduction to Rabbinic Literature*. New York: Doubleday, 1994.

Neyrey, Jerome H. *Honor and Shame in the Gospel of Matthew*. Louisville: Westminster John Knox, 1998.

Nilsson, Martin P. *Geschichte der griechischen Religion*. 2nd ed. Munich: Beck, 1961.

Nolland, John. *Gospel of Matthew: A Commentary on the Greek Text*. The New International Greek Testament Commentary. Grand Rapids: Eerdmans, 2005.

Novum Testamentum Graece (Nestle-Aland). 28th ed. Edited by Barbara Aland et al. Stuttgart: Deustche Bibelstiftung, 1979.

Osborne, Grant R. *Matthew*. Zondervan Exegetical Commentary Series on the New Testament. Grand Rapids: Zondervan, 2010.

Overman, J. Andrew. *Matthew's Gospel and Formative Judaism: The Social World of the Matthean Community*. Minneapolis: Fortress, 1990.

BIBLIOGRAPHY

Painter, John. *Just James: The Brother of Jesus in History and Tradition.* Columbia: University of South Carolina Press, 1997.

Parkes, James. *Conflict of the Church and the Synagogue: A Study in the Origins of Antisemitism.* Philadelphia: Jewish Publication Society of America, 1964.

Parsons, John J. "Reciting Kaddish: Sanctifying the Name of God." https://www.hebrew4christians. com/Prayers/Daily_Prayers/Kaddish/kaddish.html.

Perkins, Phil. "Power, Culture, and Identity in the Roman Empire." In *Experiencing Rome: Culture, Identity, and Power,* edited by Janet Huskinson, 183–212. London: Routledge, 2009.

Philo. *On the Embassy to Gaius. General Indexes.* Translated by F. H. Colson. Loeb Classical Library 379. Cambridge: Harvard University Press, 1962.

Plutarch. *Moralia, Volume VIII: Table-Talk, Books 1–6.* Translated by P. A. Clement and H. B. Hoffleit. Loeb Classical Library 424. Cambridge: Harvard University Press, 1969.

———. *Moralia, Volume IX: Table-Talk, Books 7–9. Dialogue on Love.* Translated by Edwin L. Minar et al. Loeb Classical Library 425. Cambridge: Harvard University Press, 1961.

Piotrkowski, Meron M. "Josephus on Onias and the Oniad Temple." *Jewish Studies Quarterly* 25.1 (2018) 1–16.

Porter, Stanley E. "Paul Confronts Caesar with Good News." In *Empire in the New Testament,* edited by Stanley E. Porter and Cynthia Long Westfall, 164–96. Eugene, OR: Pickwick, 2011.

Povoledo, Elisabetta. "Technology Identifies Lost Color at Roman Forum." *New York Times,* June 24, 2012. https://www.nytimes.com/2012/06/25/arts/design/menorah-on-arch-of-titus-in-roman-forum-was-rich-yellow.html.

Punt, Jeremy. "The New Testament as Political Documents." *Scriptura* 116 (2017) 1–15.

Przybylski, Benno. *Righteousness in Matthew and His World of Thought.* Cambridge: Cambridge University Press, 1980.

Quintilian. *The Instituto Oratoria of Quintilian, with an English translation.* Translated by Harold Edgeworth Butler. Cambridge: Harvard University Press, 1922.

Rajak, Tessa. "The Jewish Community and Its Boundaries." In *The Jews among Pagan and Christians: In the Roman Empire,* edited by John North et al., 9–28. London: Routledge, 1992.

Rajak, Tessa, and David Noy. "*Archisynagogoi*: Office, Title, and Social Status in the Greco-Jewish Synagogue." *Journal of Roman Studies* 83 (1993) 75-93.

Riches, John K. "The Social World of Jesus." *Interpretation* 50.4 (1996) 383–93.

Rives, James. "Religion in the Roman World." In *Experiencing Rome: Culture, Identity, and Power,* edited by Janet Huskinson, 245–76. London: Routledge, 2009.

Robbins, Vernon K. *Exploring The Texture of Texts: A Guide to Socio-rhetorical Interpretation.* Valley Forge, PA: Trinity, 1996.

———. *The Invention of Christian Discourse: From Wisdom to Apocalyptic.* Rhetoric of Religious Antiquity 1. Dorset, UK: Deo, 2009.

———. "Socio-Rhetorical Interpretation." In The Blackwell Companion to the New Testament, edited by David Aune, 192–219. Malden, MA: Wiley-Blackwell, 2010.

———. *The Tapestry of Early Christian Discourse: Rhetoric, Society, and Ideology.* New York: Routledge, 1996.

Rodgers, Cleon L., Jr., and Cleon L. Rodgers III. *The New Linguistic and Exegetical Key to the Greek New Testament.* Grand Rapids: Zondervan, 1998.

BIBLIOGRAPHY

Saldarini, Anthony J. *Matthew's Christian-Jewish Community*. Chicago: University of Chicago Press, 1994.

Schüssler Fiorenza, Elizabeth. "Rhetoricity of Revelation and Politics of Interpretation." In *The Reality of Apocalypse: Rhetoric and Politics in the Book of Revelation*, edited by David L. Barr, 243–70. Atlanta: Society of Biblical Literature, 2006.

Scott, James C. *Domination and the Arts of Resistance: Hidden Transcripts*. New Haven: Yale University Press, 1990.

Silva, Moisés, ed. "δικαιοσύνη." In *New International Dictionary of the New Testament Theology and Exegesis*, 1:723–41. Grand Rapids: Zondervan, 2014.

Slick, Matt. "Psalms of Solomon." https://carm.org/lost-books/the-psalms-of-solomon/. Accessed on 15/05/2021.

Stark, Rodney. "Antioch as the Social Situation for Matthew's Gospel." In *Social History of the Matthean Community: Cross-Disciplinary Approaches*, edited by David L. Balch, 189–210. Minneapolis: Fortress, 1991.

Suetonius. *Lives of the Caesars*. Translated by J. C. Wolfe. https://lexundria.com/suet_jul/0/r.

Tacitus. *The Complete Works of Tacitus*. Edited by Moses Hadas. Translated by Alfred John Church and William Jackson Brodribb. New York: Modern Library, 1942.

Tajfel, Henri, and John C. Turner. "An Integrative Theory of Intergroup Conflict." In *Intergroup Relations: Essential Readings*, edited by Michael A. Hogg and Dominic Abrams, 94–109. Philadelphia: Psychology, 2001.

———. "The Social Identity Theory of Intergroup Behavior." In *Psychology of Intergroup Relations*, edited by Stephen Worchel and W. G. Austin, 7–24. Chicago: Nelson-Hall, 1986.

Talbert, Charles H. *Reading the Sermon on the Mount: Character Formation and Decision Making in Matthew 5–7*. Columbia: University of South Carolina Press, 2004.

———. *Romans*. Macon, GA: Smyth & Helwys, 2002.

Tamaz, Elsa. *The Scandalous Message of James: Faith without Works Is Dead*. New York: Crossroad, 2002.

Tertullian. *The Apology of Tertullian*. Translated by William Reeve. London: Newberry, 1889.

Tesh, Sylvia N., and Bruce A. Williams. "Identity Politics, Disinterested Politics, and Environmental Justice." *Polity* 28.3 (1996) 285–305.

Thompson, Leonard L. *The Book of Revelation: Apocalypse and Empire*. Oxford: Oxford University Press, 1990.

Tilborg, S. Van. "A Form-Criticism of the Lord's Prayer." *NovTest* 17.2 (1972) 94–105.

———. *The Sermon on the Mount as an Ideological Intervention: A Reconstruction of Meaning*. Wolfeboro, NH: Van Gorcum, 1986.

Townsend, G. B. "Suetonius and His Influence." In *Latin Biography*, edited by T. A. Dorey, 79–111. London: Routledge and Paul, 1967.

Trebilco, Paul. *Outsider Designations and Boundary Construction in the New Testament: Early Christian Communities and the Formation of Group Identities*. New York: Cambridge University Press, 2017.

Vermès, Géza. *Jesus the Jew: A Historian's Reading of the Gospels*. Philadelphia: Fortress, 1981.

———. *Jesus and the World of Judaism*. Philadelpha: Fortress, 1983.

BIBLIOGRAPHY

Virgil. *Aeneid: Books 7–12. Appendix Vergiliana*. Translated by H. Rushton Fairclough. Revised by G. P. Goold. Loeb Classical Library 64. Cambridge: Harvard University Press, 1918.

———. *Eclogues. Georgics. Aeneid: Books 1–6*. Translated by H. Rushton Fairclough. Revised by G. P. Goold. Loeb Classical Library 63. Cambridge: Harvard University Press, 1916.

Wanamaker, Charles A. "Apocalypticism at Thessalonica." *Neot* 21.1 (1987) 1–10.

———. "'By the Power of God': Rhetoric and Ideology in 2 Corinthians 10–13." In *Fabrics of Discourse: Essays in Honor of Vernon K. Robbins*, edited by L. Gregory Bloomquist et al., 194–221. Harrisburg, PA: Trinity, 2003.

Westfall, Cynthia Long. "Running the Gamut: The Varied Responses to Empire in Jewish Christianity." In *Empire in the New Testament*, edited by Stanley E. Porter and Cynthia Long Westfall, 230–58. Eugene, OR: Pickwick, 2011.

Wiener, Antje. "A Theory of Contestation—A Concise Summary of Its Arguments and Concepts." *Polity* 49.1 (2017) 109–25.

Williams, Margaret. "Jews and Jewish Communities in the Roman Empire." In *Experiencing Rome: Culture, Identity, and Power in the Roman Empire*, edited by Janet Huskinson. 305–33. London: Routledge, 2009.

Wilson, Bryan R. "An Analysis of Sect Development." *American Sociological Review* 24.1 (1959) 3–15.

Winter, Bruce W. *Divine Honours for the Caesars: The First Christians' Responses*. Grand Rapid: Eerdmans, 2015.

SUBJECT INDEX

Abraham, 91
accommodation, of traditions, 16–17, 114–115
acculturation, pattern of, 46n28
Adams, Geoff W., 44, 63
Adeyemo, Tokunboh, 86
Aeneid (Virgil), 49–50, 61, 101
Africa, 46n32–47n32, 52
Agricola, Gnaeus Julius, 56
agricultural economy, 51, 52, 53, 81
Agrippa I, King, 72
Agrippa II, King, 111
Alexander, Tiberius Julius, 70–71
Allison, Dale C., 112
alms giving, 33
Althusser, 3–4
"an ancient Jewish prayer," Kaddish Prayer as, 99
Ando, Clifford, 61
anthropology, 1
anti-Jewish Ebionites, 85
Antioch of Syria, 1, 34–41, 56, 90
anxiety, forbidding, 114
apostolic Christianity, in Antioch, 38
Aquila, 91
Aramaic Kaddish prayer, Lord's Prayer echoing, 99
arch of Titus, 68–69
archisynagogos, as a patronal figure, 113
aristocracy, 42, 80, 81, 82
Aristotle (*Politics*), 79n85
assimilation, 46n28, 56, 69
Assumption of Moses, 81
audience, of Matthew, 100
author, implied, 11, 12, 31

Baasland, Ernst, 103, 104
Babylon, ultimate defeat of, 96
back-to-back relationship, 105
Baker, Coleman A., 107–108
baptism, 109
Barr, David L., 97, 97n127
Bauckham's view, disputing, 102
belief system, 109, 112
beneficence, 54, 89, 113, 114
Berger, Peter L., 14
Bernstein, Mary, 18
Betz, Hans Dieter, 28, 29
The Birth of Christianity (Crossan), 80
birth of Jesus, Isaiah prophesied, 111
bread, 30, 112, 114
"Breaking Away: New Testament Christianity's Separation from Jewish Communities" (Meeks), 83

"Caelistis," in cults of Roman Africa, 59
Caiaphas, the high priest, and his security guards, 102
calendrical inscriptions, 87
Carter, Warren, 39, 102, 111
Carthage, goddess of, 59
Case, Shirley Jackson, 31
challenges, to churches in Revelation, 96
character formation, Lord's Prayer and, 104
charismatic movements, 14
cherubim from Jerusalem, at the city gate of Antioch, 69
chiasmus, 30
chief priest, Jewish appointed by Rome, 48

SUBJECT INDEX

"chreia," teaching of, 32
Christian identity, reconstruction and legitimation of, 104–114
Christianity, 36, 38
Chua, Amy, 64
church members, supporting one another, 89
Cirafesi, Wally V., 102
circumcision, 38, 77
civic imperial cults, 64
classical authors, employing propaganda, 65
Emperor Claudius, 67
Clement of Alexandria, on 1 Peter, 94n120
closing, of Matthew's Lord's Prayer, 28–29
Cohen, Shaye C., 90
collective selfhood, in Antiquity, 19
collectivist person, in Antiquity, 17
Columella, Lucius, 48, 52
communal freedom, concern for, 105
communal memory, preserving, 107
communication, primary constituents of, 31
communicative characteristic, of the Lord's Prayer, 108
"communicative" phase, of memory, 107
community. *See* Matthean community
community prayer, Lord's Prayer characterized as, 106
comparison, observing similarities and differences, 16
conception of the self, as fluid, 19
conflict, context of, 41
The Conflict of the Church and Synagogue (Parkes), 90
contestation, 88, 89, 94
Corinthian Christians, financial support to the Jerusalem Church, 89
corruption, of the Jewish courts, 94
covenant rules, living by, 79n86
Crossan, John Dominic, 80–81
cultic associations, levels of, 64
cultural assimilation, through Romanization, 69–72
cultural categories, 10n1
cultural diversity, Huskinson's view of, 45–46

cultural identity
    formation of, 47–54
    imposition of Roman, 57
    Judean, 49, 72, 74
    Paul constructing for Jewish Christians, 91
    reconstructing through recategorization, 106–110
    in the Roman Empire, 46n30, 64–65, 117
cultural inter texture, 98, 98n1
cultural memory, 40n15, 107–108
cultural model, of prayer provided by Jesus, 32
cultural perspective, of the Lord's Prayer, 98–100
culture, 45, 98n1

Davies, W. D., 112
debt, 4, 5, 8, 24, 103
deindividuated groups, access an identity of, 71
deliverance, from evil, 30
dependence on God, for daily sustenance, 28
depersonalization, 40n15, 71
deviant Judean group, 109
diagram, plotting repeated words and phrases, 22
the Diaspora, hybrid Jewish cultural identity in, 66
Diaspora Judaism, 40, 66, 109, 110
Didymus of Alexandria, 94n120
Dio Cassius, 62, 63
diplomatic approach, resolving grievances with Rome, 115
discourse, of the early Christians, 22
distinctiveness, claimed "by promoting the myths," 46
divine status, accorded to Jesus, 43
Domination and the Arts of Resistance (Scott), 73
Domitian, 44, 61, 62
Doyle, 44
Drake, Lyndon, 3, 7–8
Du Toit, Andrie B., 103, 104–105
Duling, Dennis C., 42, 43, 44

SUBJECT INDEX

Dunn, James, 85, 90
dyadic personality, confirmed by Plutarch, 17

Eagleton, Terry, 13
early Christian communities, discourse of, 100–101
early Christian economic situation, 1 Peter and, 94
early Christianity, 10n3, 36
Ebionites, 84–85
economic aspects, of the Pauline communities, 89
economic beneficence system, 90
economic function, of Matthew's Lord's Prayer, 112–113
economic injustices, 8, 94
economic practices, religious convictions and, 51
economic principles, derived from Paul, 89
economic survival, Roman goddesses and gods and, 51
economy, 51, 89
education, 56, 70
Eisenstaedt, S. N., 42
El Djem Floor Mosaic, analysis of, 50
elite culture, 54, 56
elite households, of Rome, 55
elite qualities, in the imperial image, 57
"elite social standing," for a synagogue ruler, 113
elites, dispensing beneficence, 113
Embassy to Gaius (Philo), 75–76
embeddedness, concept of, 17
emic perspective, 9
emic rhetorical significance, 22
emperor(s), 51, 53, 54, 57, 60, 61, 67, 88, 101, 107
emperor cult, 64–65, 87, 88
"Empire: Theories, Methods, Models" (Duling), 42
epidemics, high risk of, 36
eschatological banquet, anticipation of, 112
Esler, Philip Francis, 34–35, 44, 75
essentialism, 46, 46n30

essentialist identity, embracing, 37
ethnic Judeans, in specific localities, 91
ethnic self-identity, Roman imperial theology and, 42
ethnicity, categories describing, 34
etic perspective, 9
Eusebius, on apostolic Christianity, 38
Evans, Craig A., 99
"evils," social injustices as, 19
exploitative debt, cancellation of, 5

Faulkner, Anne, 75, 83
fictive family, belonging to a, 45
fifth petition, 6
Fiorenza, 96
1 Peter, early Christian community and, 94
first-person plural pronoun, expressing a familial or communal perspective of God, 24
fiscus Judaicus (a post-73 CE temple tax), 82
Flavian dynasty, 44, 60–63, 67, 74, 82
Flavian *lex Irnitana*, or Roman Municipal Law, 60–61
"fluid conception of the self," 115
foreigners, of the individual provinces, 50
forgiveness
  from debt/sin, 30
  in Matthew 6:12, 7, 8
  needing to refer to all debts, 5
  Nel connecting to Matthew's righteousness, 6
  stressing reciprocity in, 26
"The Formation of Rabbinic Judaism" (Neusner), 66
funeral events, prayer addressing the mourners, 99

Gager, John G., 10
Gentile Christianity (Pauline communities), 84
Gentile Christians, in Rome, 86
Gentiles, 83, 90
giving, re-enforcing social cooperation, 92
gnostic Christianity, 38

SUBJECT INDEX

God
  benefaction of, 78
  care of in opposition to Roman beneficence, 114
  covenant of, 77
  entreating to act on earth as in heaven, 26, 30
  evoking the name of, 28
  exalting on earth, 29
  as the father of the community, 106
  household of, 33
  human beings' dependence on, 29
  as King, 111
  responding to injustice, 96
  will of, 26
gods, housed in Rome, 52
God's Kingdom, 78, 99, 111
Gospel narrative, on reaching out to the Gentiles, 81
Greco-Roman cultural practices of prayer, Matthew's Lord Prayer echoing, 100, 101
Greco-Roman culture, 69, 79
Greek language, 70
Greek myth, in literature in the eastern empire, 60
Greeks, on circumcision as barbaric, 77
Green, Joel B., 94n120
Grelot, Pierre, 99
group boundaries, redrawing, 16
group cohesion, reinforcing, 82, 108
group norms, 16, 17–18
group relations, 15, 119
Guelich, Robert A., 28

Hann, Robert R., 84
Hartland, Philip A., 60, 64
heavens, as the mythological place of God, 3
Hebrew, no longer intelligible to Diaspora Jews, 70
Hebrew and Judean tradition, identification with, 112
Hebrew traditions, Matthew borrowing from to contest the *prosbul*, 103
Hellenistic (Johannine Communities), 84
Herod the Great, 36

heterogeneous community, Jesus Movement as, 85
"hidden transcript," as a nonviolent response, 74
hierarchical power relations, underlying cultural identities, 65
historical inter texture, 101–102
historical Jesus, chose the terminology of debt, 7
historical perspective, of Matthew's version of the Lord's Prayer, 101–103
Homer, 100
honor, 95, 108
honor-shame language, Peter's language reversing, 95
Horsley, Richard A., 43, 86
"house of Israel," connecting petitioners to the God of Israel, 78
household, promoting an inclusive, 114, 118
household of God, Judean perceptions of, 116
"households of God," Paul focused on building, 84
human needs, attending to on earth, 29
Huskinson, Janet
  defining elite cultue, 54
  empire theory, 45
  on the floor mosaic of El Djem, 50, 52
  on individual communities as mixed, 56
hybrid identity, 42, 72–83
hyper powers, sanctioning religious pluralism and tolerance, 64

identification
  with Israel, 73, 114
  legitimating a Christian identity through, 110–114
  presenting rigid boundaries of identity, 16
identity
  connecting with the legacy of Caesar Augustus, 107
  emphasizing group-embeddedness, 18–19

SUBJECT INDEX

negotiating, 15, 16
in Rome, Diaspora Judaism, and the Jesus Movement, 41–97
identity formation
in Antiquity, 15
in the Jesus Movement, 83–97
recategorization process of, 40n15
role of society in, 12
in the Roman Empire, 42, 45–65
shaped by intergroup relations, 40n15
identity politics
of the community of Matthew, 1
construction of, 98–117
contribution of, 15–20
defining, 18, 20, 103, 106
social-evangelistic, 114–117
underlying aspects of, 119
ideological analysis, 12–15
ideological connection, between sin-forgiveness and debt-cancellation, 4
ideological intervention, Lord's Prayer as, 3
ideology
critical, 13, 15
describing group-relations, 12
general modes of, 14
pater-patria as, 107
philosophical theory of, 3–4
righteousness as, 32
Ignatius, 35, 38
ignorance, deliverance from, 19
Iliad (Homer), 100
imitation, pattern of, 46n28
imperial iconography, in sculpture and coinage, 57
imperial system, of Rome, 97
indigenous groups, in the Roman world, 46
individual, 17, 19, 20
in-group, 16, 37, 40n15
injustices, arising from the Roman Empire, 114
inner textual analysis, 11, 22–33
inner texture, 10, 12
inner voice, of a text, 11
Institutio Oratoria (Quintilian), 62

intention, determining the author's, 12
inter texture, 11, 30
"interconnected reasons," for social institutions, 14
interdisciplinary research method, 119
interpretatio, 58, 59
interpretation, 9, 41
interpreter, 22, 30
intrasectarianism, 84
introduction, to the Lord's Prayer, 27
Isaian prophetic narratives, Christian interpretation of, 111
Israel, 78, 115
Israelite identity, Jubilee as crucial for, 6

James, Epistle of, 38, 85, 93–94
Jerusalem, maintaining the Judean traditions, 73
Jesus
beneficence to his church, 89
instructions on almsgiving, prayer, and fasting, 43
joining sin and debt in his prayer, 7
Lordship of replacing the emperor, 87
orienting his disciples towards prayer, 28
"our Father" expressing his relationship with God, 25
Son of God narrative constructed by Paul, 87
as "the Son who is the image of the invisible God," 88
warning to "Beware of practicing your righteousness before men," 32
Jesus Movement, 83–97
as beneficiaries of Jesus Christ's grace, 89–90
contesting the beneficence of the Roman Empire, 113
early communities in, 93–97
flogging of members by Jewish synagogue leadership, 110
handling multi-ethnic composition, 37
as a heterogeneous community, 83, 85
interpreting the discourse of, 93

SUBJECT INDEX

Jesus Movement *(continued)*
   members of early Christian communities as, 1
   as an offshoot of Judaism, 83
   on relations with first-century CE Judaism, 41
   as sub-groups, 35
Jewish Christianity
   caught in a crossfire of hostility, 95
   focused on accepting Jesus as the Messiah, 91
   Ignatius trying to suppress, 38–39
   keeping some aspects of the Mosaic Law, 86
   Matthean communities as, 84
   wanting Gentiles to undergo circumcision, 38
Jewish Ebionites, 85
Jewish elite and aristocracy, colluded with Roman officials, 82
Jewish festivals, disrupted by seditious groups, 48
Jewish identity, 65, 66–69
Jewish liturgy, [our Father] influenced by, 25
Jewish Messiah, overcoming evil, 97
Jewish prayers, facilitating what they could not accomplish, 117
Jewish priests, allowed to offer sacrifices, 48
Jewish resistance movements, emergence of, 80
Jewish revolt, against Rome in 66-73 CE, 7
Jewish tradition, encouraging non-violent attitude, 114–115
Jews, 34, 37, 86
Jews and Christians: The Parting of the Ways (Dunn), 90
John (Gospel of), 10n2, 84
Josephus
   on the confession of King Agrippa II, 111
   on construction of the Leontopolis temple, 67
   on the Jewish population of Antioch, 34, 36
   on Judeans advocating for cultural identity, 72
   mistrust of, 48
   on observing the Sabbath, 76
   on the political significance of covenant, 77
   on the Ptolemies settling Egyptian Jews in Cyrenaica, 70
   on Rome's special treatment of the Judeans, 67
   on Titus Caesar making use of captive Jews, 74
   on the wider use of Greek language, 70
   writing the history of the Jews, 48
Jubilee, 5–7
Judaism, 25, 40–41
Judeans
   accepting Jesus as Messiah, 91
   in Antioch, 35–36
   cultural identity of, 72
   cultural practices of, 82–83
   in Diaspora, 69, 71, 82
   in Egypt, 70
   identity of, 65–83, 110
   isolation and marginalization of, 75
   leadership of, 82, 109
   liturgical tradition of, 109
   observed the Sabbath, 75–76
   religious laws of, 72
   rhetoric of covenant, 77
   in Rome, 91
   Rome's philanthropic treatment of, 67
   traditions of, 17, 113–114
judicial system, failing to defend the poor, 94
Juno, 52, 53
Jupiter
   as "Father and "King," 101
   granting the emperors powers, 62
   holding supreme authority in Virgil's myth, 61–62
   housed in Rome, 52
   sanctioned the founding of Rome, 111
   superiority of, 49
   supremacy of, 53

SUBJECT INDEX

as Supreme Patriarch and ruler of the cosmos, 101
swearing in the name of, 61
worshiping along with local gods, 52–53
justice, determined by Jesus's teaching, 88

Kaddish prayer
difference from Matthew's Lord's Prayer, 100
direct political and economic function of, 77–79
limited vision of God's household, 117, 118
Lord's Prayer echoing, 99
Kaddish Yatom, 111
Keener, Craig S., 101, 103, 112
Kingdom
function of, 110–112
word for, 24
Kingdom and Community (Gager), 10n3
Kingdom of God, 104, 115
Kittel, Gerhard, 25
Kuecker, Aaron, 34
Kurzinger, Josef, 104

Lamprecht, Liana, 29
land, aristocracy took from the peasants, 81
landholders, departure from rural fields, 52
legitimation, justifying, 14
Lenski, Gerhard, 42
life span, of less than thirty years, 36
A Light among the Gentiles (McKnight), 84
literary analysis, 2, 119
literary critics, on the rhetoric of the narrator, 31
literary performances, of words and phrases, 10
literary players, on the meaning and significance of a text, 11
literary structural content, of the Lord's Prayer, 26
loans, Jesus not forbidding, 5

local communities, 49, 53, 58–60, 65
local cultures, 60
local deities, 49, 53
local elites, 57
local shrines and monuments, 64
"Looking for Identity, Culture, and Power" (Huskinson), 45
Lord's Prayer, 98–103
affecting social evangelistic identity politics, 118
asking for God's forgiveness, 7
connection with righteousness, 33, 104
contesting Roman citizenship, 112
context of almsgiving, prayer and fasting, 104
"demanding the unqualified forgiveness of all monetary debts," 5
depicting Matthew's perspective on identity politics, 40
exemplifying correct practice, 27
as an extension of Jesus's discussion, 27
inverting the political power of the Roman emperor, 107
Lucan version of, 32
mirroring power relations of the Matthean community, 102
as a model of how to pray, 32
presenting the Matthean Jesus as the narrator, 32
promoting an inclusive household, 117
reciting of as an act of righteousness, 24
reconstructing the identity of the Matthean community, 106
reflecting social concerns of the community of Matthew, 1
social evangelistic identity politics and, 116
socio-economic and political aspects of, 118–119
"the lost sheep of Israel," narrative's focus on, 115

135

SUBJECT INDEX

loyalty, to the rule of Rome and emperor, 60
Ludi Romani festivals, 49, 52
Luke, used the Q source independently, 106
Luz, Ulrich, 104, 105

Macedonian Christians, financial contributions from, 89
Mack, Burton L., 10
Malina, Bruce J., 45, 78–79, 108
"The Man from Heaven" (Meeks), 10n2
Manichaean boundaries, emphasizing rigidity, 19–20
Mann, Michael, 45, 47
manna, 113
marginal groups, 21, 106
Martyn, J. Louis, 102
Martyn-Bauckham Johannine community hypothesis controversy, 102
Matthean community
 acquiring homesteads, 110
 attempting social evangelism, 116
 began as a Galilean Jewish sect, 84
 encouraging to seek honor from God, 105
 experiencing oppression, 102
 group relations of, 1
 intra-cultural identity of, 101
 as a Judean sectarian group or a deviant Judean group, 109
 Matthew creating an inclusive, 116
 Nel presenting as a wealthy urban community, 6
 as part of mainstream Christianity, 110
 as part of multi-ethnic society in Antioch, 36
 as part of the household of God, 105
Matthean Lord's Prayer. *See* Lord's Prayer
Matthew
 affirming Jesus's authority, 40
 constructing community identity, 33, 119
 as in-group leader of the community, 108

Lord's Prayer addressing economic injustices, 8
Lord's Prayer transforming late first century Greco-Jewish world, 117
practicing and teaching Jesus's interpretation of the Torah, 32
preserving the cultural memory of the prayer, 108
redacting Q's version of the Lord's prayer by adding "our," 101
redaction and presentation of SM (Sermon on the Mount), 105
used the Q source independently, 106
Matthew's Gospel
 composition of, 31, 76
 genealogy of, 39
 implied author and narrator treated as one, 12
 introducing Jesus as *Ima-nu-el* (God with us), 43
 on the Lord's Prayer as an "expression" or "act" of righteousness, 32
 referring to Isaiah on the release of prisoners, 5
Matthew's Gospel and Formative Judaism (Overman), 66
Maximus, Paulus Fabius, 87
May, Herbert, 83
McDonald, Lee Martin, 37
McIver, Robert K., 110
McKnight, Scot, 84
meaning, 13, 14
Meeks, Wayne A., 10, 83–84
men, honored for being courageous, 95
the Messiah, 28, 91, 97
middle, of the Lord's Prayer, 28
"the Mighty One," 74
military conscription, Judeans exempted from, 67
military security, provided by Rome, 48
millennialists, called for a cataclysmic event, 81
Minerva, 52, 53
missions, approaches to Christian in Antioch, 37, 38
modern identity politics, 19

SUBJECT INDEX

monolithic view, of Roman religion, 44
monotheism, promoting Judean, 78
monuments, commemorating defeat of the Judeans, 68
Moon, Dawne, 18, 114, 115
Moses, 80n86
mourning, Kaddish Prayer and, 78, 99
multivalent aspect, of the Lord's Prayer, 116
multivalent character, of social power, 47
multivalent response, enforcing resistance against Rome, 97
murder, of the poor by the rich, 94
mutual identity, employing, 45
mythical belief, of the divine status of the Roman Empire, 111

narrational inner texture, 30–33
narrator, role in the task of interpreting a narrative, 11
"the native tradition," 59
Natural History (Pliny), 54
negotiation, 40, 42
Nel, Marius J., 3, 4–7, 107, 112
Nero, 107
Nerva, 63
Neusner, Jacob, 66
"The New Testament as Political Documents" (Punt), 41
Neyrey, Jerome H., 45, 108
Nicholas, "a proselyte of Antioch," 37
Nilsson, Martin P., 60
Nolland, John, 28, 29
non-violent attitude, 114, 118
non-violent resistance, 42, 77, 88–89
non-violent response, to Rome, 74
non-violent stance, shifting violence to, 115
Noy, David, 113

obedience to earthly political authority, as conditional for Paul, 88
Odyssey (Homer), 79n85, 101
Old Testament, righteousness expressing a covenantal relationship, 79n85
On Agriculture (Columella), 52

opening-middle-closing inner texture, 26–30
oppression, of the Matthean community in Syria, 102–103
oppressive system, of the aristocracy, 81
Osborne, Grant R., 110–111
our Father, 25, 107, 109
out-group, 16, 37
Outsider Designations (Trebilco), 94n120
Overman, J. Andrew, 66, 115, 116
Oxford Bible Atlas (May), 83

Painter, John, 93n115
Parkes, James, 90
Parsons, John J., 78, 99
pater-patria, 107
patron-client strategy, Roman, 108
Patterns of Persuasion (Mack and Robbins), 10n1
Paul, 85–92
  on the churches in Macedonia, 92
  discouraged gnostic Christianity, 38
  engaging in nonviolent contestation, 89
  focused on the Gentile mission, 38
  on Gentiles becoming heirs of Abraham, 87, 91
  making Antioch his center, 83
  outlining political obligations, 88
  producing a set of cultural norms, beliefs and values, 86
Pauline Christianity, as a pluralism of "households," 84
Pax Romana, denigrating the role of, 78
Perkins, Phil, 51, 53–54, 89
personal identity, in Antiquity, 40n15
personification, 46, 46n32
persons, in Antiquity defining themselves, 17
Peter, 38, 94–95
Philo of Alexandria, 70
Piotrkowski, Meron M., 67
Pliny the Younger, 62
Plutarch, 17
political aspects, of the Jesus Movement, 87
political economy, 51

SUBJECT INDEX

political function
    of the Kaddish prayer, 78
    of the Lord's Prayer, 107, 111
political power of Rome, rendering
    irrelevant, 108
the poor, exploitation of by the rich, 93, 103
Porter, Stanley E., 86, 87, 88, 89, 107
portrait statutes, erected in public places, 57
Portraits of Paul (Malina and Neyrey), 17
"Post-70 Diaspora Judaism," preferable to "Formative Judaism," 66
power of God, in overcoming evil, 29
power relations, 13, 46, 50
prayers, 25, 33, 116–117
Priscilla and Aquila, 91
progression, observable in the Lord's Prayer, 24–25
prosbul, 5–7, 103
provenance, of Mathew's Gospel, 34
provinces, included in the culture of the empire, 46n32
provincial cultic associations, 64
provincial or local deity, 58
Przybylski, Benno, 79n86
Psalms of Solomon, 81–82
Ptolemies, settling Egyptian Jews in Cyrenaica, 70
public cults, in Roman colonies, 55
public display, of prayer, 33
public places, Roman, 57
public religion, 47–48
Punt, Jeremy, 41

Q source, 106
qualitative authority, 88
Quintilian, 62

Rabbinic traditions, 66, 111
Rajak, Tessa, 113
"rationalization," legitimation through, 14
Reading 1-2 Peter and Jude (Mason and Martin), 94n120
real audience, accessing, 11
real author, accessing, 11

recategorization, 15, 108
reciprocity, interpreting forgiveness of debt, 5–6
reconstruction, process of, 106
redeemed selves, creating, 19
religion, in the Roman Empire, 44, 51
religious freedom, granted by Rome, 43
religious ideas, of Paul about Diaspora Judaism, 90
religious obligations, Judeans giving precedence to, 76–77
religious rights, for the Jews in Antioch, 36
religious sects, types of, 10
repetition, of verbs and nouns, 22
repetitive-progressive inner texture, 22–26
representation, cultural identity expressed through, 46
resistance, Scott's hidden scripts of, 73–74
Revelation (Book of), 95–96, 97
rhetoric, 22, 102
rhetorical axis of communication, in inner texture, 11
rhetorical culture, early Christianity emerged in, 30
rhetorical functions, of selected concepts, 118
rhetorical/literary interpretations, 12
Riches, John K., 66
right of assembly, for religious purposes, 67
righteous ones, sons of light as, 80n86
righteousness
    applied to the Torah-complaint Jew, 79, 80
    common practices of Jewish, 41
    connecting almsgiving, prayer and fasting, 104
    contributed to the maintenance of Judean cultural identity, 79
    entering the kingdom of heaven and, 25
    explaining the fifth petition of the Lord's Prayer, 6
    hermeneutical focus on the concept of, 15

SUBJECT INDEX

Jewish sectarian groups applied three categories of words to describe, 79n86
maintaining a Judean cultural identity, 80
manifested in acts of mercy and morality, 79
Matthew's concept of, 8, 32, 117, 118
on the significance of greater, 20
suffering for, 42
of Yahweh, 79n85
risen Christ, 96, 97
ritual characteristics, of the Lord's Prayer, 107
Rives, James, 47–48, 52–53, 55, 58–59, 60
Robbins, Vernon K., 9–12, 13, 98n1
goddess Roma, 50
Roman authorities, 87
Roman citizenship, 43, 77
Roman colonies, reduplicating Rome's culture, 55
Roman culture, 57, 59, 69
Roman elites, role of, 54–58
Roman emperors. *See* emperor(s)
Roman Empire
  connecting Paul with, 86
  as historical context for early Christian discourse, 43, 44
  identities and polytheism in, 66
  identity formation in, 45–65
  motivation to maintain harmony in, 43
  multivalent nature of religion, 45
  shaping a way of life and identity in the midst of, 39
Roman Empire Theories, trends in scholarship, 42–45
Roman games, 49
Roman hegemonic power, through the Jewish aristocracy, 42
Roman imperial cult, 60
Roman imperialism, 42, 43
Roman Law, as a basis for identity, 61
Roman Municipal Law, stipulating an oath, 60–61
Roman pantheon, hierarchical character of, 78

Roman religion, 44, 51, 59
Romanization, 46, 46n30, 54, 69–72
Romans, 42–43, 77, 87
Rome
  acceptance of religious cults by local communities, 44
  assisted in the maintenance of Judean cultural identity, 48–49
  belonging among the hyper powers, 64
  as the center of religious and economic matters, 48
  centrality of in matters of identity, 60
  facilitated the social aspect of religion, 49
  formation of cultural identity, 47–54
  as more honorable and powerful than the provinces, 51
  multivalent function of demonstrated by *Ludi Romani*, 54
  not imposing deities on Roman provinces, 58
  obeying when administering justice, 88
  reasonably tolerant of local religions, 48

Sabbath observance, 75, 76
sacred references, traditionalizing of, 14
salvation, proclamation for both Jews and Gentiles, 36
scholarship
  Biblical, 41
  New Testament, 3–8, 42–45
Scott, James C., 73–74
Sebastoi (members of the imperial family), 64
second Jerusalem temple, 73, 74, 115
secret place, prayer done in, 33
"Sect Development" (Wilson), 10n4
sects, types of, 10n4
self-awareness, depending on group embeddedness, 17
self-esteem, desire to maintain, 16
self-individuation, in Antiquity, 17
self-representation, 46–47

SUBJECT INDEX

semantic analysis, 22–33
   sentence diagram guiding, 23
"Senatorial hatred of Domitian," 63
Septuagint, creating, 70
Sermon on the Mount (SM), 3, 42, 105
shame-honor values, intertexture reflecting, 103
"shared set of assumptions and experiences," helping detect cultural values, 45
Shimoneh Esreh prayer, 32, 109, 111, 117, 118
Silva, Moisés, 79n85
slave of Jesus Christ, Paul as, 88, 91
slavery, to a Gentile master, 71
slaves, 94, 95
SM (Sermon on the Mount), 3, 42, 105
small forgiveness/release, practiced by Jesus' followers, 7
social chaos, Antioch experiencing, 36
social codes category, of social knowledge, 100
social concerns, of the community of Matthew, 1
social context, 14, 15
social environment, conducive for worship and socio-economic engagement, 48
social evangelistic identity politics, 114–117
social evangelistic movement mode, 19
social events, religion in Rome as, 49
social good, 114, 115–116, 118
social history, Nel engaging to study the Lord's Prayer, 6
social identity, 12, 16, 40n15
social intertexture, achieving, 100
social knowledge, categories of, 100
social memory theory, 40n15
social movement evangelism mode, 19–20
social perspective, of Matthew's version of the Lord's Prayer, 100–101
social phenomena, categories of, 13
social power, 13, 47, 61
social relations, 101

social scientific models, modern interpretive dynamics utilizing, 2
social separation, between Judaism and Christianity as inevitable, 90
social setting, 34–97
social tensions, high risk of, 36
social values, Paul's conviction of Christian, 89
social-economic environment, in Antioch, 36
Social-Identity Theory, 40
socialization, process of, 71
socio-economic elites, propagated Roman culture, 57
socio-economic ethics, of Matthew's gospel, 4
sociological and anthropological perspectives, of the Lord's Prayer, 1
sociology, 1
Socio-rhetorical Analysis Theory, 1, 20, 119
Socio-rhetorical Analytic Theory (SRAT), 9–21, 69, 118
"Socio-rhetorical Interpretation" (Robbins), 10n6
Socio-rhetorical Interpretation (SRI), 9–12, 27, 31
sovereignty, of God over evil on earth, 29
Spain, as an economic partner with Rome, 52
speech and action, explaining ideology, 13
"speech and language," contestation observed in, 88
Stark, Rodney, 36
Statius, Publius, 62
stereotypical categories, bearing connotations, 15–16
subjects, of identity politics, 18
submission, depicting Christ, 95
subordinate group, employing non-violent response, 74
Suetonius, Gaius, 44, 61, 62–63, 67, 103
suffering, for righteousness, 42
superimposing, Roman belief systems, 59
superior group, identification with, 40n15

SUBJECT INDEX

superordinate category, 16, 108
superordinate identity, 37, 73, 92, 116
superordinate identity category, constructing, 117, 118
suppression, of Judean cultural identity, 71
supremacy, of Rome over local deities, 53
symbolic forms, 13, 14
symbols, of power relations and power structures, 14
synagogue communities, Matthew discrediting, 39
synagogue rulers, qualifications for, 113
synagogues, 70, 84
Syrian Antioch. *See* Antioch of Syria

Tacitus, 48, 53, 56, 62, 63
Talbert, Charles H., 85–86
Tamaz, Elsa, 93n115
tasks, of ideological analysis, 14
teacher of righteousness, presenting Jesus as, 32
temple of Jerusalem, subjugation of, 68
temptation, as a means of God's wisdom, 29
Tertullian, 58
Tesh, Sylvia, 18
text
   analysis of, 10
   biblical, 2, 10
   interpreters of, 12
   layers of meaning, 93
   written, 30–31
Thompson, Leonard L., 13, 44, 62, 96
Tiberius, 53, 67
Tiberius Julius Alexander, 70
Tilborg, Sjef van, 3–4
Titus, 67, 68, 74
toga, adopting, 56
Torah, 74, 75, 76, 91
Torah-conditioned righteousness, 80
town councils, formed from the political elite, 55
trade, in Rome during *Ludi Romani*, 52
Trajan, 63, 103

transformation, focus on the individual level of, 19
transformation agenda, of social movement evangelism, 115
Trebilco, Paul, 94n120
"the true Israel," reclaiming Israel's covenant privileges, 115–116
"Typology of cultures," categories of, 10n1

"Undivided Way" (Hann), 84
"universalization," legitimation justified through, 14
"us-them" binary, context of, 40n15

Varro, Marcus, 52
verbs, imperative in the Lord's Prayer, 25
Vermès, Géza, 25
Vespasian, 48, 62, 67
vilification, 16
violent attitudes, initiating transformation, 115
Virgil, 48, 49–50, 51, 61
virginal birth of Jesus, Ignatius's references to, 36

Wanamaker, Charles A., 13–14
warning, Lord's Prayer introduced by, 24
"The Ways That Parted" (Cohen), 90
"we" petitions, in the Matthean Lord's Prayer, 105
Weber, Max, 14
Westfall, Cynthia Long, 93, 94, 95, 96
"who is in heaven," emphasizing distance, 25
Williams, Bruce A., 18
Williams, Margaret, 67–68, 71, 77
Wilson, Bryan R., 10
Winter, Bruce W., 38
Wittfogel, Karl, 42
women, 94, 95
Woolf, 44
works of Law, Paul's position on, 109–110
written texts, as additional tools, 30–31

ANCIENT SOURCES INDEX

Old Testament

Genesis

17:1–27	91
34:14	75

Exodus

13:19	80n86
16	112, 113
20:1–26	91
21:2–6	7
23:7	79n85
23:10–11	7

Leviticus

7:15	80n86
21:3	80n86
25	5, 103
25:10	6

Numbers

16:1–24	76

Deuteronomy

7:3–4	75
15:1–3	103
15:1–6	7

Job

1:12	29
2:6	29
7–17	29
42:26	29

Psalms

33:5 LXX	79n85

Isaiah

6:5	111
9:5–6	111
9:6–7	111
24:23	111
52:7	111
61:1	7
61:1–7	5

Jeremiah

34:8–17	7
34:8–22	91

Ezekiel

46:17	7

Daniel

	95

Hosea

6:6	39

Deuterocanonical Books

4 Ezra

10:21–23 NRSV	74

Psalms of Solomon

	48, 81
4.1–6	81–82

Pseudepigrapha (Old Testament)

2 Baruch

	74n77, 75
5.1	74
29.8	112
85.3–5	74

Assumption of Moses

10	81

Dead Sea Scrolls

1QH (Thanksgiving Hymns)

4:38	79n86
7:26–33	79n86
7.12	79n86

1QM (War Scroll)

	79n86

Ancient Jewish Writers

Josephus

34, 48, 49, 70, 83

Antiquity of the Jews

6.1–18	77
12.119	36
13.62–73	67
14.213–25	67
16.163	76
16.169–70	73
16.27–28	72
20.100	70

Against Apion

2.44	70

Wars of the Jews

2.342–44	115
2.390	111
2.427	7
7.421–36	67
7.43	36
7.96	74
16.16	67

Rabbinic Works

Kaddish Prayer	77, 99, 117
Kaddish Yatom	111

Mishnah

Mishna Sota

9.15	25

Sifra A. M pq

13:194.2.1	111

Sifra Behuq. pq.

8:269.2.3	111

Sifre to Deuteronomy

313:1.3	111
323:1.2	111

Yoma

8.9	25

Shimoneh Esreh

111, 117

ANCIENT SOURCES INDEX

New Testament

Matthew

	76, 84, 85
1:1–11	34
1:1–17	39
1:2	39
1:18–22	36
1:18–25	40
1:23	43, 100
3:10	109
3:13–17	40
4:1–11	40
4:17	39
4:24	38
5:1	109, 116
5:1–2	43
5:3–12	32, 39, 41
5–7	105
5:10	24
5:12	7
5:17	110
5:17–20	25, 41, 43
5:19	24, 25
5:20	8, 20, 24, 25, 33, 40, 104, 117
5:21–48	41
5:25–26	5, 6
5:40	6
5:42	6
5:43–48	42
6:1	24, 25, 27, 32, 107
6:1–2	105
6:1–4	33
6:1–8	27
6:1–18	41, 43, 104
6:1–33	8
6:2	33, 41
6:2–4	104
6:5	41
6:5–7	20, 33
6:5–15	104
6:7	33
6:7–8	27
6:7–15	105
6:7a	27
6:7b	27
6:8	27
6:9	3, 4, 23, 24, 26, 29, 32, 33, 99, 101, 106, 107, 108, 111, 116
6:9–10	108, 114
6:9–13	1, 2, 20, 23, 25, 26, 32, 114
6:9–15	108
6:9a	27
6:9b–10b	28
6:9b–13	27
6:10	23, 24, 26, 102, 110–112, 115
6:10a	24
6:10b	24
6:11	23, 24, 28, 30, 112–114
6:11–13	26, 28, 33, 108
6:12	4, 5, 6, 7, 23, 24, 26, 28, 30, 33, 103, 112
6:13	24, 28, 30
6:13a	29
6:13b	28
6:14–15	5, 6, 8
6:16–18	104
6:19–23	15
6:19–24	7
6:25	114
6:25–33	114, 117
6:33	4, 6, 24, 104
7–8	33
7:23	109
8:11	112
8:18	116
9:36	116
10:5–6	34, 38, 84
10:6	115, 116
10:17	102, 110
12:3–5	39
12:21	116
12:50	33
13:1–35	24
13:36	116
18:23–35	5, 6
20:26	95

ANCIENT SOURCES INDEX

Matthew (continued)

21:46	116
23	41
23:1–34	40
24:30–31	42
25:32	116
25:32–46	42
26:3	102
26:57–62	102
28:18–20	115
28:19	116
28:19–20	34, 38, 81, 84

Mark

1:8	109
6:37–42	113
14:36	25

Luke

	39, 101
3:9	109
9:13–17	113
11:1	32
11:1–4	113
11:2	106
11:2–4	99
13:14	113
22:28–30	112

John

	84, 85, 97
9:22	84, 102
12:42	102
16:2	102

Acts

	36
1:5	109
2–11	83
2:37–38	109

6:7	37
11:26	36
18:1–2	67
18:2–3	91
18:18	113

Romans

	85, 86
1:1	88, 91
1:3	87
4	87, 91
4:1–3	91
6:4	109
7:12–16	91
8:23	112
13	88
13:1	88
13:1–7	86, 87, 88
13:1–13	88
15:25–29	36
16:22	88

1 Corinthians

	86

2 Corinthians

	86
2:1–5	89
8	86, 89, 90
8:8–13	92
8:9	89

Galatians

	39
2:6	110
2:7–8	38
2:11–14	36, 38
2:12–17	90
2:14	38
2:15–16	37
2:15–21	38

Ephesians

1:13–14	112
2:11–12	84

Colossians

1:15	88

Hebrews

6:4–5	112

James

	85, 92, 93, 95
2:2	93, 94
2:6	94
2:15	93
4:13–17	93n115, 94
5:1–6	93n115, 94
5:4, 6	94
5:6	94

1 Peter

	85, 94, 94n120, 95
2:18–25	94, 95
3:1–6	95
3:1–17	94
3:8—4:19	94

Revelation

	93, 95
2:8–9	96
2:9–10	96
2:13	96
2:14	96
2:20	96
2:20–23	96
3:17–18	96
6:1—8:1	96
12–13	97
18	96
18:2	96
21:24	96

Early Christian Writings

Eusebius

Church History

3.3.5	38
3.36.2–3	38

Ignatius

	34

Epistle to the Magnesians

8.1	38
10	39
10:2–5	38

Epistle to the Philadelphians

6.1	38–39

Epistle to the Smyrnaeans

1.1–2	36
2.1—4.1	38

Epistle to the Trallians

10.1	38

Greco–Roman Literature

Agricola

	55, 56

Aristotle

Politics	79n85

Cicero

	55

Columella, Lucius

	48, 52, 55

ANCIENT SOURCES INDEX

On Agriculture
1.5–13   52

Dio Cassius
62

Roman History
67.2.1   63

Dionysius of Halicarnassus
48

Homer
Illiad   100
Odyssey   79n85
1.2   101

Horace
48

lex Irnitana
26   61

Livy
48

Philo of Alexandria
70

Embassy to Gaius
158   75–76

Pliny the Elder
Natural History   54

Pliny the Younger
62

Plutarch
Dialogue on Love   17
338–39   17n28

Quintilian
Institutio Oratoria
10.1.91   62

Statius, Publius
62

Suetonius, Gaius
49, 62, 65

Claudius
25.4   67
Domitian
13.2   44, 61, 103
14.1   62–63

Tacitus
48, 63

Agricola   57
21   56
Annals
4.6   53
Histories
4.51   62

ANCIENT SOURCES INDEX

Tertullian

Apology
24:3–4   57

Virgil

48, 55

Aeneid
49, 59
1.254   61
1.65   101
2.648   101
6.852   49
10.2   101

Georgics
1.26–37   51

www.ingramcontent.com/pod-product-compliance
Lightning Source LLC
Chambersburg PA
CBHW051941160426
43198CB00013B/2243